The Women Who Would Not Die

ALSO BY UDDIPANA GOSWAMI

Fiction

No Ghosts in This City (2014)

Poetry

We Called the River Red (2010)

Green Tin Trunk (2014)

Non-fiction

Gendering Peace in Violent Peripheries (2023)

Making Peace Mutually: Perspectives from Assam (Co-edited, 2021)

Conflict and Reconciliation: The Politics of Ethnicity in Assam (2014)

Indira Goswami: Passion and the Pain (Edited, 2012)

Folklore

Where We Come From, Where We Go: Tales from the Seven Sisters (2015)

The Women Who Would Not Die

Stories

UDDIPANA GOSWAMI

SPEAKING TIGER

SPEAKING TIGER BOOKS LLP
125A, Ground Floor, Shahpur Jat, near Asiad Village,
New Delhi 110049

First published by Speaking Tiger Books in 2024

A version of the following stories first appeared in *No Ghosts in This City* (Zubaan 2014). They have been edited and expanded for this collection by the author: *Andolan, Sin and Retribution, I Thought I Knew My Ma, I Don't Love Sam, Colours, This Is How We Lived*

ISBN: 978-93-5447-917-5
eISBN: 978-93-5447-958-8

10 9 8 7 6 5 4 3 2 1

Typeset in Sabon LT Std by SŪRYA, New Delhi
Printed at Chaman Enterprises, New Delhi

For Mita Bose. She was the kind of teacher every student should have.

Even when I was too young to know myself, she saw me. She shaped my mind with her scholarship and wisdom. She recognized my pain because she, too, was in pain. She shared her vulnerabilities with me so I, too, could be strong.

Contents

Andolan

Our Barbari is a small town with a big population. Over the years, it has grown into a commercial hub of the kind that dots most of mofussil Assam, intricately linked to the larger market but little known outside of its own district. The reasons why Barbari developed its commercial nature are many, but the most important is the small tea garden right outside our town. Or to put it more accurately, our town grew just outside this garden, Kalguri, which is the original name of the area that was taken over by the British for the tea plantation.

On the infrequent evenings that he sat with us around the winter fire, or stretched out in the courtyard on the camp bed while us kids took turns fanning him as everyone sweated it out in the summer, my father would tell us tales about Barbari, Kalguri, and all the people that lived here. To our young minds, he was the custodian of the town's living history, having been among its founders, and now its elder and community leader. It was probably from these tales that I developed my interest in studying history as I pieced together the chronicles of Kalguri and the tales of Barbari. *Deuta* told us that until the mid-1900s, there were only a handful of educated middle-class Axamiyā people employed by the British owners to work as babus in the plantation offices. He was one of them. The rest of the middle- and lower-rung white-collar employees were almost entirely brought in from neighbouring East Bengal. The upper-rung—the management—was primarily white. The Bengali babus were familiar with the colonial administrative machinery, having been in the system longer than us. When Assam became a part of the British Raj a century after the rest of India, their job market expanded. The perks of migrating to an unknown land to live among us—the savage lot—who spoke a corrupted version of their own superior language included spacious living quarters and a not-so meagre salary. So they came, the prospective babus, to the many tea plantations of Assam and lived in these quarters for generations as the jobs rolled down from father to son.

'That Bolen, he sat in the same chair that his father's backside had warmed for twenty years. And now there's Bolen's son. Three generations have farted in that chair, maybe we'll match their record!' *Deuta* had laughed his deep-throated, tobacco-infused laugh when his own son, my brother Akhyay da, joined the estate as a clerk.

For *Deuta,* the annals of Barbari and Kalguri were his history, and his history became ours, even if we inherited it in different ways, my brothers and I.

Kalguri, like all tea gardens, was a fortress in itself, and like every fortress, had its own rings of security. On the outermost fringes were the labour lines where the expendable workers were housed in shanties. The clerical and administrative staff—the babus—lived in sturdy, well-maintained quarters among the precious, picturesque tea bushes. And at the centre of it all was the management, entirely white, though towards the end of British rule, a little brown also entered the mix. The most privileged of the lot, the rich white owners, of course, lived among their own kind, in their faraway countries. The tiny sliver of the vast profits that these owners invested in our parts went into ensuring tight security and isolation from the outside world for the white managers, as well as for the expensive factory equipment and priceless tea. Barbed wires and guarded, forbidding gates sealed off the money-making machines and mechanisms from the world outside that was inhabited by the teeming natives whom they both loathed and feared, as all oppressors loathe and fear those whom they oppress.

Within a couple of decades after India's independence, the white managers were gradually replaced by ones with brown skin, but the tea estate remained a fortress, largely cut off from the real world. This isolation and insularity became a habit of those who lived within its limits.

'It could have become our life too,' *Deuta* would say, and sometimes take us to see the old house: the mud and bamboo hut he built with his own two hands in Nepali Basti, a 31-acre stretch of wasteland that he reclaimed and turned into his private botanical garden, planting any and every fruit and flowering tree he could collect. He had moved out of the tea estate and into this hut so he could dedicate more time and energy to growing his landholdings and adding to his labour force of agriculturalists. Then, he transported brick and mortar all the way from Guwahati to build the sprawling house where he brought Ma as a new bride and in which my brothers and I were born.

'I wanted for you to grow up in society, among our

people,' *Deuta* told us. And because there weren't enough of 'our' people—Axamiyā-speaking caste Hindus—he convinced people from his native village to come and settle in the vast tracts of uncultivated lands lying waste around the town. So busy were they building homesteads and cultivating their huge farms, that my parents and their kin hardly ever heard the murmurs of discontent that were growing louder in the centers of power. For not long after Assam joined the independent union of Indian states, political turmoil had begun spreading through our land. The people were angry because the promises of equal respect, political dignity, and equitable rights had been made when the new nation state was being constructed, but just a few years down the line, these were revealed to have been reserved for the people of the heartlands, while the peripheral people like those of us in Assam were alienated and exploited.

This turmoil wasn't discussed in our home while we were growing up—it didn't really create any ripples in our self-sufficient, self-contented community—and what I came to know of it, I learned only after I had finished school and left Barbari. When I did, I also realized that Barbari had remained similarly unperturbed by the anti-colonial andolans and communist peasant rebellions that had raged across India earlier and eventually reached Assam. Through it all, my parents had clung on to the life of domestic ease and social influence they had built for themselves in Barbari. They refused to look beyond their immediate world and kept their focus on ensuring that they moved up in life as much as they could without inviting trouble.

When we were growing up, we sometimes heard murmurs of malcontent from other places of more significance, about how our people had never really won freedom and had merely been handed over by the colonial British overlords to our Indian oppressors. We weren't much bothered, though, because we didn't feel oppressed—our days were carefree enough and spent swimming in the Krishnai river, fishing in its waters, climbing trees, jumping on haystacks and riding the elephants my father owned. It was fun to speak the language of the mahouts—*aget, boit*—and watch the elephants obey. No oppressor bothered us, brown or white. Now that the British Raj was over, our school textbooks only identified those with white skin as oppressors. The manager and a couple of senior staff at Kalguri were still British—sometimes American—but they rarely emerged from their sprawling bungalows and no one we knew seemed to mind them. The only time we saw them was when they came into town to make guest appearances for the community during Bihu and Puja celebrations. One year, my eldest brother, Rames da, went up to the manager, Johnny sahib, and shook his hand on a dare when the manager was being led out of the Bihu pandal by our father. Rames da did not wash his right hand for a week after, and even ate his meals with his left hand. That was the closest any of us children had gotten to any white man, and Rames da was our hero for years after.

The rest of us only got to watch from a distance, surreptitiously, as though looking boldly, directly, was somehow transgressive. Sometimes, we would stealthily peek in through the hedges around the manager's bungalow while making our way back home after plucking tea flowers for our cook so that she could make us fritters that tasted like fried eggs. The peepholes in the thick hedges would give us fragments with which our young minds put together a dreamlike montage: a deep blue swimming pool quietly shimmering in the evening light, or a tennis court waiting for the floodlights to be turned on, before the white masters and the occasional brown sahib and memsahib in tight white shorts and skirts came out to swim and play or relax after a long day at work—'*Lord, what monstrous work!*' a student leader would say sarcastically when I joined college, '*Dealing with incompetent natives in the offices and drunk savages on the plantation. And oh, the heat and the damp!*'

Deuta caught us snooping one day. He made us run back home alongside his bicycle, our ears still red and ringing from how hard he had pulled them.

Many years later, Akhyay da reminded us of that evening as he dried off his sweat by the fire in the courtyard. I was studying in Guwahati and had come home for a weekend. We were sitting around the fire, warming the palms of our hands. Akhyay da had just returned from playing tennis with the new assistant manager at the Kalguri estate, a young chap from Delhi who was fresh out of college and had taken up this job on a whim because he loved adventure and exploring unknown lands.

'Remember how scared *Deuta* was for us when he saw us lurking outside the bungalow, peeking at the tennis courts? Well, I play on those courts now, *bhoni*. We are no longer the *chotto lok*!'

The pride in Akhyay da's voice made me bristle. I hadn't realized until that evening how much college had changed me. '*Hoine*?' I heard myself say. 'Really? Maybe they don't call us "low lives" anymore because the Bengali babus who taught them to treat us that way don't run everything anymore, and maybe there are more of us Axamiyā people in the estate administration now. But doesn't your Indian assistant manager friend still call you Asami? You may think it's a joke, being called a criminal just because their foreign tongues can't pronounce the name of your people, but don't think for a minute that they are not laughing at you behind your back. You are still only a clerk to them.'

'You have become too serious after going to Guwahati, *bhoni*. I *am* a clerk. And they *did* always call us Asami, but we never felt insulted before!'

Akhyay da sounded more amused than offended by my newfound political awareness. But Ma never found anything funny.

'We sent you to college to study, not talk politics like all the other kids these days. We were never low lives, nobody ever called us *chotto lok*—they wouldn't dare. And Asami or Axamiyā, how does it matter? If it wasn't for your father's plantation job, you wouldn't have had such a privileged upbringing. You wouldn't be studying in Guwahati, you would be married off like Bhikhu's sister and dead in childbirth by now.'

'*You* were never called *chotto lok* to your face, Ma, because you were Deka *dangoria*'s wife. *We* were called that when we went cycling through the estate with our friends and they didn't know we were *Deuta*'s children. And just because Suren dadu's daughter-in-law brings you your favourite Bengali novels from Calcutta every time she goes home, it doesn't mean he did not insult every Axamiyā writer ever during our literature club meets in school. Three generations in Assam, and now even their old country does not exist, but does anyone in their family speak a word of Axamiyā? Do they ever eat our food without complaining how "simple" and tasteless it is?'

'*Bhoni*, enough! Let's go get some potatoes to roast in the fire,' Akhyay da intervened before Ma could respond to my outburst and dragged me by my hand to the kitchen. When we returned with two armloads of potatoes, Ma had left the courtyard fireside. She would be overseeing dinner preparations soon, and I didn't need to worry about her rebuke anymore: I was leaving for college next morning, and she wouldn't have the heart to scold me before the long bus journey.

The rest of the siblings sat around the fire and talked about the good old days, and I listened to their stories with an uneasy feeling that kept growing and squeezing my heart till my chest hurt. I had felt the same unease during the Students' Forum meeting in September to which my roommate Laboni had dragged me. The forum leaders were discussing an action plan to assert our Axamiyā rights and identity that they said had been threatened in our own land since Assam became a part of India. The outsiders from all over India—the Biharis and Bengalis and Marwaris—and those not from India—the East Bengalis who had their own country, Bangladesh, by the time I reached college—had taken control of our politics, economy, culture. All of us Axamiyā, they announced, must now work unitedly, whether we were tribals or non-tribals, to send these foreigners back where they came from.

I did not understand most of what was being said,

especially because I grew up with all the Biharis and Hindu Bengalis and Muslim Bengalis and Marwaris and Nepalis and could not imagine a Barbari without these people. And when I spoke to Laboni later that night, both of us lying broodingly in the dark on our beds, I kept telling her stories about my childhood.

Suren dadu had featured in many of those stories. Up until that night, I had thought my childhood fear of him was only the fear that every child nursed against the school principal who haunted our dreams, where a failed test or late arrival would end in a visit to his room. As I narrated my tales of terror to Laboni now, I was suddenly unravelling deeper and more insidious fears and a constant sense of being lowly and unworthy that came from being who I was, not as a student, but as an Axamiyā student in Barbari MV School where the principal was an enlightened, educated Bengali whose elder brother, Bolen dadu, was the head clerk—the *boro* babu—in the plantation, and who dictated what play our community theatre would stage or which famous Calcutta artist would be invited to the next Durga Puja programme.

While Suren dadu lived in the town and directed its cultural life, Bolen dadu lived with his family inside the plantation, in their official quarters, and desperately preserved their original, East Bengali Hindu way of life. And this despite the fact that their connection with the homeland grew more and more tenuous every day with the distance in time and with all the political upheavals happening there after the British colonizers left and the Pakistani neo-colonizers took over following India's Partition. As their language and culture were disparaged over there—their identity erased even from the new name for their homeland: East Pakistan—they were asserting it more and more emphatically over here. Living within the fortified boundaries of the tea plantation suited the Bengali babus well since anti-outsider, anti-immigrant sentiments were growing steadily all over Assam. These sentiments could not hurt them inside the plantation where they were a rung above all the rest of us, even though they used to be second-class citizens under the white masters. And since India's Independence, these Bengali babus were the ones running the show, albeit from behind the curtains.

As more and more Indians from the mainland gained control of the tea estates from the white masters, they turned to the Bengali babus to keep the estates running the same way as before. The brown sahibs had a different skin colour, but they slipped easily into the way of life of their white predecessors. This was the life we saw, frozen in time, through our peepholes in the thick hedges of the estate. For a long time, only the Bengali babu had access to the life on the inside, as a visitor with special rights; now even Akhyay da was invited in occasionally. Things were changing, even though they were still the same: Ma and Akhyay da didn't seem to know or care that these changes did nothing for us—we were still the *chotto lok* in our own land.

Before Akhyay da, my father had been the rare exception, the Axamiyā babu who had access to the white sahib, and later to his brown successor. But *Deuta* had found the plantation life restricting. He continued working for the estate but ventured out of its confines early in his career. Like him, a few other enterprising Axamiyā also reclaimed the plentiful forest lands surrounding the plantation. Eventually, they became masters of vast tracts of land, virtual zamindars.

And just like my father, when they'd had their fill, they brought people from their native villages in other parts of Assam and gave them land—there was plenty lying 'waste'—and settled them in the area, which then came to be known as Barbari. To work on their immense land holdings, these new landlords employed the local tribal population who had lived in the area for centuries before the tea garden was set up. These were mostly Bodo people who had been employed as workers by the tea garden owners before the shrewd capitalists realized that it would be cheaper and easier to get indentured labour from other tribal areas in mainland India. The Bodo labourers were hard-working but often intractable. Besides, they had their own agricultural land to fall back upon and could not be coerced to stay against their will if they wanted to leave.

The new labour force comprised poverty-stricken tribals from Central and Eastern India who were bought and sold like cattle by and for the British plantation owners. They were made to live virtually like slaves within the tea estate in subhuman conditions, and it continued this way for generations. A few lucky ones among them were sometimes relieved of their slave duties and allowed to leave their plantation jobs. But they had nowhere to go—their original homeland in the forests of Central India was a forgotten dream—and they opted to settle down in the areas surrounding Barbari. Eventually, these ex-tea tribals, or Baganiya, as they were called, set up their own villages. Some of them managed to reclaim some wasteland, others were employed by the relatively prosperous people of Barbari as menial labourers in their households or agricultural fields.

This small Baganiya population could not, however,

meet the huge demand for agriculturists in the vast amounts of land reclaimed by my father and his peers. Some Bihari and Nepali people heard of the new opportunities and they came to Barbari looking for employment. Each new wave of migrants worked for the original settlers but also reclaimed small tracts of land for themselves. The demand for more agriculturists grew, and so, finally, the community leaders decided to allow migrant peasants from East Bengal, to come and settle in the region.

Deuta said Aminul mama first suggested bringing these peasants to Barbari during one of their community meetings. He was a *matabbar*, a very influential man within his community, who had settled down in the Kalguri area shortly after the first wave of peasant migration from East Bengal was started by the British administrators sometime in the early 1900s. Some said he had been in the area even before the tea garden was set up. Others claimed he had grabbed his immense tracts of land around the same time that the tea garden was set up. He had helped *Deuta* and the other landowners of Barbari-Kalguri as well, when they were clearing out the forests for cultivation and, since then, he had remained involved with the town's many developments. He was often a part of the evening addas of the community leaders in their club house which, really, was an outhouse *Deuta* had constructed in our homestead.

Aminul mama's suggestion had appealed to *Deuta* who valued his counsel. The peasants from East Bengal were poor and landless, broken by centuries of zamindari oppression and ravaged by natural disasters. They were eager to move to any place that offered them an opportunity to till the soil. Their white-collar compatriots were loathed and revered, as those in power tend to be. But the peasants were powerless, the lowest of the low. So, they were tolerated and allowed to come in by the upper and middle classes who, truth be told, needed them. The East Bengali peasants, it was widely known, could turn any land productive; they were natural agriculturalists. And unlike their countrymen in white-collar jobs, these peasants were willing to subsume their native language and culture in the local. Their aim was economic survival: they left behind their original homes in search of land and livelihood, both of which had been in short supply. There was no going back, and if that meant that they had to accept the lowest rung in the social hierarchy of their adopted homes, they were willing to do so.

There was still, however, the problem of their religion. 'Deka, these peasants are Muslims. How can we allow them to settle here? We will be accused of harbouring enemies of our faith,' some of the other community leaders of Barbari had objected in Aminul mama's absence when *Deuta* said he was inclined to accept his proposal.

'Don't worry,' he had reassured them. 'There are ways of dealing with these *Miyā*. They are not like the Hindu Bengalis, they will not try to prove they are superior to us. They will be subservient and if we are tactful, we can control them. Besides, they will live in their own clusters and villages. We need not worry about their religious customs vitiating our environment. I have gathered this much from my conversations with Aminul.'

My father had thus convinced them, and they allowed him to approach Aminul mama to bring some of his people from East Bengal. He brought them in large numbers by river and land, and soon we had quite a few *Miyā* villages in the area. They began working in our fields and Aminul mama also employed some of them himself. Everyone benefitted from the arrangement, but it was Aminul mama's gain that began to bother some residents of Barbari. Especially the Marwari mahajan, Moti, who claimed that people like my *Deuta* were naïve to trust Aminul mama who had sinister plans of bringing his country people to our fertile area and taking it over, making us all Muslims.

Moti was always Moti mahajan to us; we only called him chacha when face-to-face with him. Whenever we went to his shop to buy mitha paan for Ma (and beg for unpaid extras for ourselves to stealthily chew on when Ma wasn't around), Moti would remind us how trusting *Deuta* was, but also 'what a great man. Barbari would be the backwaters without him!'

Moti was one of the three Marwari merchants of the Barbari-Kalguri area who had set up shop selling daily essentials to the tea garden labourers, factory workers and officers. Gradually their businesses had grown and now they operated not only the rice and sugar mills in the area—the raw materials for which came from Aminul mama's fields and the fields owned by my father and the other Axamiyā people of Barbari—but also a garment shop, a small hotel, and a tiny cinema hall with an ancient projector. The Marwaris were also the area's usurers, lending money at huge interest rates to the cash-poor tribals and Baganiya people. To repay these loans that never seemed to add up in the mahajan's books, the poor workers and farmers would hand over their small land holdings or work as unpaid labourers for the usurer for generations. Or they would take out another loan from the Bengali Hindu trader. Also from

East Bengal, these adventurous Bengalis had come to Barbari when word travelled about the new economic niches created by the developing township. They opened up paan shops and grocery stores and lent money and acquired land and free labour and provided various services to the town. Soon we had a Bengali homeopath, the only doctor in town, a Bengali jewellery-maker who was the craze of all the women, and a Bengali cycle mechanic.

All these people made up the diverse population of Barbari and its surrounding areas. As a result, our town took on quite a cosmopolitan nature by the time my brothers and I were born in the 1950s. As the population grew, so did the need for infrastructure. A cooperative market and, after that, a cooperative bank were also set up. Not long after Indian Independence, a panchayat office was also set up and my father was panchayat president for many years running. He was the undisputed leader of the local community, although he was always mindful about including Talukdar *khura,* Aminul mama, Rajani *bordeuta,* Shishir kaku, and all the other prominent people of Barbari in every decision he took.

All these people together approached the district administration for a primary school that was later upgraded to an MV school while we were students. After I'd left Barbari, it became a high school and today, I hear it is a higher secondary school. It is to the MV school that all of us went, whether we were Axamiyā or Bodo or *Miyā* or Bihari or Bengali or Baganiya or Nepali. I had friends from all the communities and none of us had any idea then that we were all studying together only because we did not have another option. Had there been more than one school in our small town, perhaps the affluent people like my parents would have sent us to one school and the poorer parents of the tribal and immigrant children would have sent them to another. We would have remained separated then as we were to be separated soon after we left school, and slotted into different ranks and files as dictated by social norms. Since we were forced together, however, everybody celebrated Bihu and everybody danced to the dhak during Durga Puja. When the Baganiya had their Kali Puja in December, everybody went to the all-night open-air cinema shows held in their basti. One year, our school Saraswati Puja president was a *Miyā,* Aminul mama's son Khairul. We all had great fun together and did not know that we were any different from each other.

This was the way things were among us children. Among the grown-ups, of course, it was a different story. When Aminul mama came home, he knew that he could not come inside and sit in our drawing room. He and my father would discuss their business affairs sitting on the veranda or in the club house. There was a separate cup and saucer reserved for him, but at least he did not have to wash them himself before leaving. Others like Abdul chacha, who was the president of the cooperative market but much less powerful than Aminul mama, would have to. As would all the Bodo, Nepali, Bihari, and Baganiya visitors to our house; my mother insisted on it.

'Or else,' she told my father, 'they cannot set foot in my house.'

Only the Bengali Hindus were considered clean enough to eat from the same plates as us. My mother often sent across food she had cooked to kakima, the matriarch of the upper-caste East Bengali Hindu family next door, and whenever kakima cooked something she knew any of us liked, she would call out to one of us children and pass the food through a gap in the fence.

When we visited any of our friends' homes, we were never expected to wash our own cups and plates. My mother never ate in anybody else's house but we would gladly eat the duck eggs and drink the buffalo milk offered at Khairul's house, or the pigeon meat at Sabita's house—she was a Bodo and the daughter of our school teacher, Ramendra Musahary. Of course, we could not eat the pork that Sabita's family made because it was forbidden in our community, nor could we eat any kind of meat at our Muslim friends' homes for fear it might be contaminated; they cooked beef in the same utensils, we were warned at home. And I was always the rule follower. But I came to know later that Akhyay da would not only eat pork and beef with his Baganiya and *Miyā* friends but also drink the *jou* with his Bodo friends and *haria* with the Baganiya. Alcohol was another taboo at home, but it seems not just Akhyay da, but all my elder brothers, had developed a taste for the different varieties of indigenous rice beer early in life. But so long as my mother did not know, they were safe.

❧

Once MV school was over, Barbari had nothing left to offer by way of education. My father, however, insisted that all his children should get a proper education and not just complete high school but also go as far as university. Three of my elder brothers had left home for Guwahati once they completed MV school in Barbari. Only Akhyay da resisted. He wanted to stay close to home and enrolled in Kalguri

Higher Secondary School and cycled to and from school every day. He scraped through high school and struggled with his higher secondary studies, managing to pass after two attempts. Thereafter, he decided to give up studies altogether, much to our parents' dismay, and eventually joined the tea estate office as clerk when my father retired.

I left home to join high school in Guwahati and where none of my brothers managed to go beyond their undergraduate studies, I got an MA from Gauhati University and joined as a lecturer of History in B Baruah College before getting married. My father insisted that his only daughter, the brightest of his children, should marry somebody who was intellectually her equal. He found me a professor at the Gauhati University and with implicit faith in his judgement, I married a man I had barely met twice. On our wedding day, I pledged before the sacred fire to be his wife not just in this life, but for quite a few more to come.

My husband was a kind man who did not make me feel the want of anything. Anything, that is, except his company. Within a few years of our marriage, he became one of the most well-known folklorists of Assam, and people everywhere sought him out and invited him to meetings and public functions and seminars. When he was not attending these meetings and functions and seminars, he was conducting fieldwork in some interior village and writing and publishing his research papers. I was proud of his achievements, and in awe of them, but guiltily, sometimes, I found myself wishing he would spare some time for me and the children: we had two and they only saw their father between his fieldtrips and public engagements. I had to make up for his absence by confining my work to my classroom teaching, so that any time that I spent outside of the college was time dedicated to the children. Once, very long ago, I had dreamed of working toward a PhD but that dream faded away as I realized that any given family can only contain one researcher at a time.

'Why don't you take the kids with you on one of your field visits?' I asked him once as he was leaving on a short field trip. 'They will have your company and also learn from seeing the outside world.'

He looked at me incredulously. 'Do you have any idea what these places are like where I go?'

I didn't understand and when he saw the confusion on my face, my normally taciturn husband spoke as he hadn't done in all the years of our marriage.

'It is best they don't know this "outside world" as you call it, and may it remain forever outside for them,' he said, stuffing a few more pens into his fabric bag. 'Do you want them to see how man behaves towards his fellow men in the name of religion and ethnicity? Yes, I study the customs and cultures of these societies, and they are all very beautiful. People appreciate what I write because I write about their richness. But when I am amidst them, I also see their paranoid fear of the other and the hatred they each carry for the other in their hearts. In themselves, they are good people, but between them, they are deeply divided. Why else have we had riots every decade since Independence, Jeuti?'

He paused long enough to sling his bag over his left shoulder and pick up his overnight bag. As he stepped out into the veranda, I remained standing by the front door that I'd held open for him since asking him the question that set him off like this. Before stepping into the driveway, he turned and said, 'It is best for our children to remain in the city where at least in this home and in their school they are not made aware every single day of the differences among their classmates and friends. Let them continue living in this bubble for as long as they can, because this bubble is going to burst. I can see it coming, a tide of blood. The hatred we've been nursing against each other in our breasts will engulf us, soon.'

I was too shocked by the uncharacteristically long outburst to respond immediately, and by the time I had recovered, he had got into the car and driven away. I shut the door and sat down on the sofa.

There were so many things I wanted to tell my husband, and so many ways I could set the record straight. After all, did I not grow up in Barbari? Did we not all live in harmony there? True, communal and ethnic riots had taken place everywhere else in Assam but never in Barbari. *Deuta* had died a few years ago, but people like Aminul mama and Shishir kaku, though very old now, were still respected. They still led their respective communities and had always maintained peace in the area even when the neighbouring regions were in ferment. No, Barbari would never be like any of the other places of Assam, and I told my husband as much the next night when he returned home and I determinedly picked up the threads of our unfinished conversation of the previous morning.

'How long has it been since you were back there, Jeuti?' he asked me calmly.

'Why, we went there last summer!'

'No, I mean how long has it been since you were *really* there? As a part of the place and the community? You go there with the children once or twice a year and stay for a few days and visit your relatives and old friends. But do you still belong there? Do you care to find out what lies beneath the surface? And among the friends that you visit, do you still go to Bhikhu's house in the Baganiya basti? Or to Abdul's house in the *Miyā* village? Would you even recognize Abdul now if he stood before you with his long beard and checkered lungi? Would you allow Bhikhu into your house here today if he were to decide to come and see his old school friend? Could he sit at our nice table and eat with us?'

That stung, more so because I suspected it wasn't untrue. Somewhere in the journey to a university degree, a highly regarded teaching job, and a nice, neat house in the city, I had changed. Had I become my mother? Or had I always been like that, deep inside? Either way, I wasn't ready to confront the truth just yet.

'Maybe, maybe not,' I deflected. 'That's not the point. I'm not talking about myself. I left that place a long time ago. What I am saying is that you should not think that disparities will always lead to violence. I think I am a better person for knowing and growing up among so many different kinds of people. I just wanted you to take our children with you so that they could also see all the diversity in the world outside, feel the richness of it, and learn to appreciate it.'

'You could have done that all those times we were in Barbari, couldn't you? Learning about the outside world does not always have to be a clinical experience. It could be lived. It should be felt. This morning I told you what I felt, and I am telling you now, I have also felt the same foreboding of doom in Barbari.' He turned his back to me and immediately fell asleep.

It was true that he knew more about Barbari now than I ever did. Every time we went there, he would only wait for a cup of tea before mounting my father's old bicycle and pedalling away into the nearby villages or to the Baganiya basti with his bag hanging from one shoulder. His constant companions—a notebook and an assortment of pens—were always in the bag. He would only come back home for meals because he knew my mother would be extremely hurt if he didn't. Sometimes, if he was off-duty, Akhyay da would give him a ride on his motorcycle and take him to meet newer people. At those times, they would not return till late at night and, when they did, they would both be drunk and singing happily. My mother had long reconciled herself to Akhyay da's ways. As for my husband, she was too much in awe of his reputation and too smug in the social status that came with having a famous and learned son-in-law to complain about his drinking. If anything, she had taken to defending him now whenever I complained.

'He has to work among these people and gather information. How will he do that if he does not sit down with them and take what is offered? As it is these tribals are so hot-headed, they will take offence at the slightest thing. If he said no and they took it as an insult, how would he write his books?'

'And if he eats beef with the *Miyā*? Would you be okay with that too?' I would challenge her.

'I know my son-in-law. He will never do anything of that sort,' she would maintain obstinately.

I was not so sure myself, but there was very little I could do. He was forever away among these people and even if he did eat the meat they offered or drank alcohol with them, so long as he did not bring those things home, I preferred not to comment. And he never did, so I was fine with it.

I was not fine, however, with what he was saying now: that Barbari might be heading towards trouble. The children's summer vacations were approaching and although we had skipped Barbari during the winter break to take them to Darjeeling, they were clamouring to go there for the summer. My husband was never unenthusiastic about going to Barbari, and so we drove down two days after the vacations started. We had intended the trip to be a surprise for my mother and had not called ahead to inform her. We should have, for we were just a few kilometers from Kalguri when we sensed that something was wrong. The roads were lined with armed paramilitary policemen standing guard every few metres on the highway, and several armoured trucks were parked by the roadside. We stopped in front of one of the policemen and asked him what had happened. He said a young Baganiya boy had been found murdered last night in Kalguri and any day now, ethnic riots were likely to break out.

My husband did not say 'I told you so'; he was not that kind of person. But I suddenly felt my head reeling. Who was this young man, did I know him? Who had killed him? When we reached Barbari, Akhyay da was livid.

'Why didn't you call before leaving Guwahati? This whole place has been tense for a while now—we did not want to alarm you, so we said nothing. But we would never have allowed you to come if we had known. As it is, I was thinking of sending Ma, Matu, and the kids to Guwahati. But now with this boy killed, there is no guarantee that violence will not spill on to the highway. How will you go back? It is bad enough that we are trapped here and now you have come too!'

That night, as we sat in the courtyard fanning ourselves and talking of the good old days, we found ourselves whispering although there was nobody to overhear our conversation. Akhyay da and my husband had gone to a peace meeting that had been called hastily to bring the warring communities to a dialogue and possibly to a mutually acceptable settlement that would prevent bloodshed. Such meetings had worked in the past when my father and his contemporaries had presided over them. Sometimes through reasoning and sometimes through coercion, they had brought the parties in conflict to peace. But most of them were dead now, and Aminul mama and Shishir kaku were too old to be dragged into a violent situation; their families would not let them leave home.

'This wouldn't have happened in the days your father led the community. Those were the days when people knew subservience and accepted authority. Today, everyone has rights, everyone needs power, everyone wants to be the leader. How will society function this way? If everyone were to be king, who would rule over whom?'

My mother's tirade about king and community reminded me of an incident in school one day. The first class that day was Sanskrit. Shashtri saar was our Sanskrit teacher and everybody was afraid of him. I was late because Rames dada was running a fever and Ma had sent me to fetch a homeopathic medicine for him, but the doctor had not yet opened shop. I'd had to go to his house and request him to deliver the medicine at home after he had had his bath, and then I had run all the way to school. I was breathless and trembling from head to toe as I stood at the classroom door, not daring to open my mouth and ask for permission to enter. But Shashtri saar saw me standing there and stopped the lesson.

'Ah, maharani, come in, come in! So you decided to grace us with your presence after all!'

I felt like dying but walked in anyway, only to find that there were no empty seats. When he saw me hovering near the wall and realized why, he turned his attention to Bhikhu who was sitting in the front row.

'*Oi lora,* get up. Go stand against the wall and let Jeuti sit.'

Bhikhu did not budge. Shashtri saar threw his book at Bhikhu and asked him to get up again. He did get up this time, and mumbling something under his breath, came towards the wall.

'What was that?' Shashtri saar asked him.

'Nothing, saar,' Bhikhu mumbled.

'How can it be nothing, I heard you say something. Out with it!'

'*She's* the one who is late, why punish me?' Bhikhu said tremulously.

Immediately as he heard that, Shashtri saar flew into a rage and charged at Bhikhu and gave him a resounding slap.

'You coolie dog! You dare question my authority? Do you know who she is, you two-bit Baganiya? She is the daughter of the king of this town. If it were not for him, you would not be here studying but picking tea leaves all your life like your parents and their parents before them. So when I say you need to vacate your seat for her, you need to vacate your seat for her. Do you understand?'

Bhikhu now quietly made his way toward me.

Shashtri saar turned to me. 'You! Why are you still standing there? Come here and sit down. I don't have all day.'

As I walked nearer to him, however, he saw that I was crying. I did not want him to treat Bhikhu that way. Bhikhu was my friend, and although it had hurt to hear him say that I should be punished, I realized that he was right. I was late, I should be the one standing against the wall, not him.

'What happened to you now? Why are *you* crying? He got the beating, he is made to stand against the wall, and you are crying?'

I could not say anything and started bawling now. At this point, Shashtri saar gave up and walked out of the classroom. Later, I went up to Bhikhu and apologized, but he turned his back and walked away.

The other day my husband had asked me if I would allow Bhikhu to enter my house in Guwahati now if he suddenly showed up. I had to admit I wouldn't. But it was the same Bhikhu for whom I had shed those tears so many years back. What had changed? Nothing, perhaps. I could not speak out in protest then and put my foot down in front of Shashtri saar. I would not speak out now and admit to my husband that he was right. That we had sown the seeds of discontent from the very beginning, but wanted to believe that we were not to blame. We never set fire to anything, but we provided the fuel, and now they were lighting the matches everywhere. Even in Barbari.

Akhyay da and my husband returned a few hours before dawn when they saw that it was futile to try and broker peace. The riots were inevitable. However, the commanding officer of the paramilitary police force assured them that if we could drive out before sunrise, we should be safely out of the conflict zone by daybreak. Matu bou, my sister-in-law, quickly bundled up the children while I helped my mother collect her valuables. Akhyay da stayed behind and the rest of us drove away.

As we crossed Kalguri on our way out, I saw black smoke rising out from behind a clump of trees a little way off the highway. It might be houses burning; maybe the riots had started already. Or it could be the young man's cremation. I could not shake off the feeling that it was Bhikhu—my old classmate Bhikhu, some other Baganiya boy named Bhikhu, it didn't matter which Bhikhu. Whoever it was, I was responsible for his death and the many deaths that would follow once we were safely on our way to Guwahati and the rioting began.

I Thought I Knew My Ma

I thought I could see my Ma in a green and white polka-dotted frock, sitting on her bed beside the window. Looking out at the night sky, trying to capture the full moon between two pink wild roses blooming on the old creeper that curled around the bars of the window. I thought I could hear her sigh as she smiled to herself dreaming of a tall dark-haired man, clutching a microphone and singing in a gravelly voice on the Bihu stage, under another full moon. She was thinking: 'I will marry him when I grow up, and *Deuta* should have no opposition to that because although he is a Muslim, he is an artiste, like *Deuta*.' *Koka*, my grandfather—her *Deuta*—always said that literature and art should be the only religions people were ever allowed to practice.

They were her religions too, although she had also told *Koka* that loving flowers should be another religion. She was practicing her religion now, loving the flowers, letting them hold the moon in their bosom. The flowers shifted slightly in the breeze, and the moon was hidden for a moment. At that same moment, a shadow passed over her face. She was wishing the artiste had not been a Muslim, because although art, literature, and loving flowers should be the only religions, in Barbari, where they lived, Hindu and Muslim were the only religions anyone spoke about, as if no other faith mattered, no other way to live and love.

The Muslims in Barbari were mostly immigrants, and unlike our cultured and educated indigenous Muslims, *Aita* said, the immigrants fought over land and cut each other up at the slightest provocation and gave birth to lots and lots of children 'so that they can grab some more of our land.' *Aita* herself had eleven children, of whom my Ma was the youngest. But she reasoned that *Koka* was very rich, and they could afford to have as many children as *Aita* could bear.

Aita was proud she could bear her husband so many children. *Koka*, of course, never knew how they were raised because *Aita* kept them under her control and also, he was hardly ever home. If he was not supervising his vast land holding, he was settling some dispute in the village of which he and three or four other men were undisputed patriarchs. They had set up Barbari by clearing the forests and settling people from their old villages, and bringing Muslim agriculturists to work on their fields. In the evenings, *Koka* would be rehearsing for the next play the Rangmahal club would stage: he was their chief patron and often, the lead actor. When there was no play, Choudhury *koka,* Sirajuddin *koka,* Dambaru mama and everybody else would get together and discuss poetry or music. Sometimes, if the artiste was not travelling with his troupe, he would come and sing in the entrance hall of their sprawling home which—*Aita* often complained—*Koka* had transformed into a theatre hall. 'My *batghar* is now a *natghar*,' she would say.

When the sounds of the rehearsals started reaching the main house, and *Aita* had retreated into the kitchen, my

Ma would sneak away from her study table and run to the *batghar*. It was through these rehearsals that Ma had grown so close to *Koka*; he liked that one of his children was interested in the arts. And *Koka* forever for her remained the artiste, the lover of literature, and the man who always quoted Chandraprasad: *Xundarar aradhanai jibanar khel:* the sport of life is the worship of the Beautiful. Sometimes, the image of the Beautiful conjured up in her mind would be that of her father, sometimes of the tall, dark-haired artiste. She only ever wanted to be the silent worshipper.

I thought I could sense my Ma's bewilderment when she was forced to come and live in Guwahati. I thought I could measure her reluctance. She had not wanted to come, but *Koka* had insisted she get a better education than he ever did: 'Study English literature, because it will teach you to appreciate how beautiful life is.'

She had heard from him that pain could be beautiful, and after the death of the artiste—some said from drinking too much, but she never believed them—she had often felt that loss could be as precious as love. Without anybody knowing it, she had stolen the teacup kept aside for him (*Aita* always insisted that no Muslim could drink from the same cups as the family did) and hidden it in her trunk under her bed. Although she hardly ever took it out of there, she liked to think: 'This is the cup that runneth over with my grief.' She left behind the cup when she went to Guwahati and once when she came home for the holidays, she did not notice that it was gone from her trunk. Just like the artiste's cup, many things had slowly slipped away from her unnoticed, but not her shyness, her solitude, and her love of the Beautiful, reinforced now from studying the English Romantic poets.

The silken slender threads of a mournful flute found her one day at her hostel window when she was once again toying with the moon. They were floating in from the direction of the boys' hostel, and she was immediately in love once again. Her artiste had come back to life and she had found something to hold dear in this city where everything seemed daunting, everybody intimidating.

'Majnixa xar pai xunisane ketiyaba ketekir hiya bhaga mat?' her favourite poet had once asked. She felt the wailing of the bird, that the poet had heard in the middle of the night, must have aroused the same pain, the same heartbreak as the music of the flute now did in her.

Sometimes she wondered who it was that could weave such sorrowful magic; often, she told herself the magic was enough, the magician incidental. And she would not have known who it was, if he had not played the same melancholy notes during the College Day celebrations.

That day, as she sat there in the auditorium with her friends, she suddenly, for a moment, went back to her old bed at home and could smell the wild roses at her window. But she was grown up now, and knew she could not fall in love with, and dream of marrying, someone just because they pierced her heart with so much pain.

She knew now what marriage entailed and could foretell how *Aita* and Koka would both react if they only knew she was in love with a tribal boy. *Koka* would perhaps understand the love and devotion, but she knew well enough now that abstract religions of the heart had nothing to do with institutional religions people practiced in their everyday lives, and even *Koka* would not accept such a social ignominy as his daughter marrying a tribal boy.

Oh, the tribals have converted to Hinduism all right, but they do still eat pork and drink alcohol. And although her elder brothers often went hunting in the reserved forest nearby and brought home deer meat almost every time, and maybe even ate wild pigs and buffaloes on the sly, pork—and, of course, beef—were taboo at home. And all the men of the house, including *Koka,* only drank alcohol in secret, never socially like the tribals did.

She had been shocked the day she found a bottle of rum in her father's safe which he had accidentally left open. She had never told anybody about it, and had later accepted that although drinking alcohol was bad, it was a weakness even the strongest of men must sometimes give in to. And then, they do say artistes need alcohol to express their art. Was her flute player drunk now?

Suddenly, she came back to herself and found herself sitting in the auditorium surrounded by an applauding audience and blushed. The performance had ended, and she wished she could look at him for some time longer. Since she could not do that now, she started sitting at the back of the classroom every day and watching shyly, guiltily, his profile on the boys' side of the room. And waiting for the evenings when she could listen to him playing the flute.

She made believe that he played only for her, because only she could make his pain her own.

One day, instead of the music, she heard a huge commotion from the direction of the boys' hostel. Some of the more adventurous girls in the hostel went over to the warden's and brought back the news that the tribal boys had started a rebellion of sorts. They would no longer eat in the Second Dining Hall, they wanted to eat with the upper caste Hindu boys in the First Dining Hall. There was a little violence, and some of the boys on both sides had been injured.

From the next day, she did not hear him playing the flute anymore. The news was some of the boys in the hostel had been rusticated for indiscipline; he was one of them. Some of the other girls who had taken to openly declaring their adoration of him ever since the College Day, proudly proclaimed that at least his sacrifice had set in motion a change that would be good for society.

She wanted to cry because she hated it when they spoke about him as though he could ever belong to anybody but her.

I thought I felt my Ma's trepidation the day she got married. I thought I knew how her tears were both of sorrow at leaving her parents' home and also the fear of the unknown life she was about to start by marrying *Deuta*. Her only consolation was that *Koka* had himself chosen *Deuta* to be her husband, and she knew he would never make a wrong choice for her.

She had barely met *Deuta* a few times before the wedding but she had read his novel and imagined he would be like

Pramathes, the protagonist, who was a social activist and stood for all that was true, right and good. She was also a bit worried that if he was as good as Pramathes, she might not live up to his expectations.

But her sense of inadequacy began to disappear as she started learning a few lessons about life in the daily grind of married life. The first of these lessons was that a man who was too good to be true should not get married. Unaware of his duties to his family, *Deuta* indeed turned out to be like Pramathes, consumed with a desire to cleanse society of its evils and injustices. Perhaps it was something in the air in those days, but many other people like *Deuta* also thought they could do this, and very naively they all joined the Asom Andolan—that massive civil unrest that turned our society upside down for nearly six years. It was a well-intentioned movement which a few self-serving people hijacked and turned into one that polarized our society, alienating the dominant Hindus from all Muslims as well as tribals.

People like my *Deuta* who had joined the movement because they wanted to fight for the rights of the 'sons of the soil' did not realize this until it was too late. And then, when they did, they ended up as bitter defeated crusaders who remained forever afterwards cynical about any change in society. *Deuta* could never get over it, and he changed entirely, kept strictly to his textbooks and teachings, pretty much banishing whatever was left of Pramathes from his person.

Meanwhile, my Ma had already given up two of her favourite preoccupations, because early in the marriage, she had realized that it would not do for both partners to immerse themselves in art and literature, or there would be nobody to run the house, what with *Deuta* also possessing, at the same time, an unbending social conscience. Since the same realization had not come to *Deuta*, it was my Ma who had had to relinquish.

She did, however, keep her third religion alive, that of loving flowers. She had a huge garden with many different kinds of flowers to which she was more attached than to *Deuta*. When I was born, she named me Pahi—flower petal. I thought I could sense her disappointment when she realized I had not turned out to be as delicate, as pliant, or as attached to her as her flowers.

I was more attached to *Deuta* who would sometimes, only for me, come out of his cynical shell and recount the fervour with which his generation had wanted to 'save our nation and identity'. Another generation was, at that moment in history, trying to do the same with guns and explosives and failing miserably, defeated by ideological poverty.

Growing up amidst all this and knowing what had gone before, I started believing that mass movements and armed insurgencies led nowhere. Revolution had to begin at the individual level, and I started my own little rebellions. I began by renouncing the Brahminism I was born into. I took to eating beef and pork with friends, and later, travelling to and writing about places my mother would only have heard of, or my one-time social activist father would never have been acquainted with, where the people—who he had once thought he was fighting for—really lived.

There, getting drunk on rice beer, we discussed ethnic reconciliation and religious tolerance, deliberated on blueprints of a future society without conflicts. And I came to believe that I was in love, with an indigenous Muslim boy who spoke with the same passion about the same things I believed in.

I had thought my Ma would be my worst enemy at this juncture. That *Deuta* would be the one who would understand.

But it was *Deuta* who very subtly blackmailed me into agreeing to marry Bordoloi *khura's* son who lives in Bangalore. He stopped eating, and sat on his easy chair in the veranda for hours with a wounded look, the book on his lap open at the same page for a week.

I gave in and said I would marry whoever he picked for me. And I did. But not before I realized that my mother was on my side.

When the wedding preparations were underway, *Deuta* perked up, left his easy chair and even his books for a few weeks to have the invitations printed, the grounds cleared, the shamiana fixed, and the cooking and catering attended to. Between endless visits to the weavers and the jewellery makers and the beauty parlour, I could not get away. I wanted desperately to go meet my boyfriend so I could explain to him why I had abandoned my rebellion and betrayed the social revolution we had dreamed of together. Then, a few days before the wedding, Bandini came to see me and told me the truth. I had never felt so much pain before.

I thought my Ma would not understand this pain—which I believed was so different from hers—because she said nothing when I broke the news to the family that I had given up on the revolution. I thought she was silent only because

Deuta had said all that she would have wanted to say about the hollowness of the golden dream we had both, father and daughter, dreamt in different ways at different historical moments for the collective, restorative future of our society.

But she came and sat beside me on my bed later and ran her fingers through my hair as I recounted to her how the love of my life had been going around town heaping accusations of hypocrisy and elitism on me. 'And what are you?' Bandini had confronted him because she knew that all the while that he had been with me, he had been sleeping with another woman as well. When she came to see me, she said I was well rid of him, and I knew I was, but along with him, I had also lost my faith in myself, and my world and my rebellion and my beliefs had all come crashing down.

It was then, as I lay crying, surrounded by the unbearable devastation raining down on all sides, that I suddenly saw my Ma amidst the ruins. As she told me of her own lost loves, of the Muslim artiste and the tribal boy, I saw that she felt my pain, that she was, indeed, made of pain.

And it was then, for the first time in my life, that I thought I should get to know her the way she must have been.

Sin and Retribution

I froze in the middle of a carefully calibrated stroke of my *da*. The sleek iron machete felt heavy in my hands as I strained to hear the words above the wailing. Somebody was shouting, '*Oi* run, run! CRP!'

Maybe it was Ramen.

But how could it be? How could the Central Reserve Police be there already? Not even half of Nayagram had been covered yet, and it was a small village, just a cluster of twenty huts or so.

'*Ha Hari*! *Pola pola!* Who informed them?'

I recognized Pulakes's voice not very far from me.

'Must be Ratan. *Salla*, son-of-a-pig humanist!' I wheezed.

It is not an easy task cutting up live human beings. And these were strong hardy peasants—with their multiple wives and the plentiful children that they reproduced endlessly.

'Imagine,' Saikia saar had told us last week at headquarters, 'here is a village of twenty families, but with a population of 200! They breed like animals and take from us what is ours by right.'

He told us they had grown strong because we let them. We allowed them for so many years to be bred, fed and made strong on food that should have been ours, cultivating land that was ours, usurping our livelihood and threatening our identity, proliferating and gaining strength every day.

No, it was not an easy task at all.

It had not been an easy task planning the attack either. We had to catch them unawares, unarmed. We had been told these peasants were dangerous when their meagre possessions were threatened, and very obstinate about clinging on to their pathetic lives. We had been told not to underestimate them—they were survivors who had lived through famines and floods, military oppression and brutal massacres. They had come to our land determined to survive, but if we wanted to put an end to their silent invasion, we would have to exterminate them. We should, however, never, never underestimate them.

Thus it was that we had planned the attack for tonight. It was Eid and the whole day, the people of Nayagram had been feasting. At least the few who had stayed behind—around seventy; the rest had gone back to their old villages for the festivities. Nayagram was a newly established village, the land had only just been reclaimed five years back by Bordoloi *mohori* of our Na Pam village and in these five years, he had encouraged these filthy peasants also to come and settle. They were, after all, cheap labour for the vast stretches of land that he had claimed for his own—it helped to be a government appointed land revenue official. He had had to give a few bighas of land to the *matabbar* of the immigrants, Kasem Ali, to persuade him to resettle the peasants from their old villages, but that was a small price to pay. Kasem Ali must have had very little problem convincing these twenty families to move. Always starving, relentlessly breeding, they are anyway forever on the lookout for newer lands to encroach.

'Before long, we will no longer be Axamiyā. We will all be *Miyā*, all Muslims. Our names will have Ali or Begum attached to them, and we will be speaking their filthy tongue. Our long-suffering Axami *āi*, our dear motherland, will be swallowed whole by these land-hungry invaders. Theirs is a strategic expansion, a Bengalization of our land. Soon, we will become a part of their country, Bangladesh. Mother India cannot save us: her power centers are too far away to heed us, or our desperate pleas for help. We must defend our own hearth and home, our own language and culture!'

Saikia saar's words had been ringing in my ears since last week, and killing these usurpers had seemed like the only way to save our motherland and our national identity. The others also must have been similarly inspired, but it was not until Pulakes blurted out loud, 'Let's kill those bastards!' that the rest of us admitted we were thinking the same.

Saikia saar had just left after our afternoon tea session. In the short time that we had set up our village level branch of the Assam Nationalist Youth League, we had begun to refer to the tiny one-room structure we had erected with bamboo cut down from Bordoloi *mohori*'s backyard as headquarters. Saikia saar had walked into headquarters one afternoon a couple of years back to have tea with us while we were wracking our brains about what to do next, having played ten games of carrom since the morning and endless rounds of cards. He was the headmaster of the Dhaniram Saikia Secondary School built in the memory of his late father in the nearby Purani Pam village, besides being the headman of the same village. Always dressed in a pristine white dhuti and cotton shirts stitched from handwoven cloth, he had a reputation of being the most learned man in Purani Pam and everybody revered him.

Even Bordoloi *mohori*, who was the richest man in the area, could not take any decision without at least informing Saikia saar. It was with Saikia saar's blessing that he had resettled the lands near Purani Pam village with his entire clan and scores of people besides from the neighbouring villages of his native Nalbari district. That is how our village of Na Pam had come up a decade or so ago. Slowly, the *mohori* had begun to reclaim more and more land around the village so that Nayagram had to come up next. Since Purani Pam, or 'old settlement', was the name of the original village in the area, the later villages that grew up around it came to have the prefixes 'Na' and 'Naya', respectively, the Axamiyā and Bengali words for 'new'.

We got to know all this from Saikia saar. He was a repository of knowledge and we learnt more from him about our own identity, history, culture, and politics than we ever could from our textbooks in college. As his visits to our headquarters became more and more frequent, we came to look at him more and more as our advisor and guide, our ideologue. He told us that he was not too happy about bringing the immigrants to our area, but Bordoloi *mohori* had been adamant.

'What could I do? He is the richest man, I am a simple teacher.'

Saikia saar was such a humble man! We knew he was quite well-to-do and owned a lot of land himself, although of course, Bordoloi *mohori* owned much, much more. Nobody, however, could have been richer in experience and knowledge than Saikia saar. But he never had any airs about him: he was always soft-spoken, unassuming, and as time went by, we realized how much he had influenced us for the better.

He not only instilled in us a pride of being Axamiyā but also made us realize the importance of self-help. He said we, the Axamiyā people, had always been laidback, and so the British could come and enslave us. After the British left, it was now the Bangladeshis who were occupying our land and usurping our livelihood. Our forefathers had never allowed the Muslim rulers to occupy our land, but now, we were giving up to these lowly peasants without a fight. We were too unconcerned about our own welfare even as the Indian government showed a step-motherly attitude towards us and turned a blind eye to our woes.

What Saikia saar told us was, of course, nothing new—we had been reading about all this in newspapers and our nationalist magazines for a few years now. All over Assam, there was a growing wave of resentment against the Bangladeshi invaders. We also heard of isolated incidents here and there where protests had taken place urging the government to take steps to safeguard our land and identity and oust the immigrants. At places, these protests had also turned violent. What Saikia saar did was to make us realize that these were not incidents that we could afford to just read about and forget. If people all over the state were rising in protest, we should also do our bit. We were also, after all, not unaffected by the rampant immigration.

'Look at our own village,' he reminded us. 'We were two Axamiyā clusters living peacefully—the old and the new, Purani Pam and Na Pam—and then came the Muslims and set up a 'Nayagram'. Why should we allow them to enter our midst, I ask you? Before long, you will see them multiplying by hundreds, taking over our economy, vitiating our language. Our boys will soon take to eating beef and we will all be forced to turn Muslims. Is that what you want? It is a good thing you have taken the initiative of starting this village level branch of the League. You are bright boys, you are our future. You will have to lead the resistance in our village. We are old people, worthless. Our days are over. But you will have to preserve the Axamiyā identity for your progeny.'

Finally, we had a sense of purpose. Finally, we realized that we could do something about the sorry plight of our motherland and make our lives worthwhile. Everywhere in Assam, we kept hearing about so many martyrs these days, young men like us who were killed while confronting the immigrants and the government that looked elsewhere even as millions of them crossed the international border illegally every day. The Indian armed forces and the Central Reserve Police forces were all in league with these immigrants, always safeguarding them. So many of our Axamiyā boys fell prey to their bullets and batons. Only in our village, we were doing nothing. We were still silent. Then last week, after Pulakes spoke our minds, we decided it was time for action. Just a few days ago, an entire village of immigrants had been massacred by 'unknown assailants' in our adjoining district. Everybody had been horrified that something like this had happened so close to home, but not many had shown much sympathy for the immigrants.

'They will breed back like animals again,' all said.

It was easy to come to terms with these incidents if we did not think of those killed as human beings, and that was what everybody did. We also did that while we made our frenzied plans for the day of Eid. We hardly had five days' time between Pulakes's outburst and Eid, the day when we knew we could safely attack. There would be very few people in the village and all of them tired from the festivities. Despite the incidents elsewhere in Assam, the Nayagram immigrants were least expecting any violence to break out in their village. After all, they had the patronage of the richest man in the area, and despite the threat posed by the League members in major immigrant inhabited districts of Assam, our village level branch had never been quite so active. Though I am not proud of it, I guess we were seen as a bunch of unemployed idlers who had started the branch for want of anything better to do. Even my own father with whom I speak less and less every day complains incessantly how I waste my days with the other loafers, playing cards and carrom and drawing up a huge tab at Bhola's tea stall.

'But that will act to our advantage, don't you see?' Ramen deduced; he had always been the brightest of us. 'The element of surprise is essential in such enterprises. Nobody will expect us to take matters into our own hands in this way, and so nobody will suspect our involvement in it as well.'

Ramen fancied himself well-read in literature about guerilla tactics. He had borrowed a Mao Tse Tung book from his brother Ratan when we started planning and flipped through its pages. Ratan had asked a lot of questions when he saw his good-for-nothing younger brother sitting with the book in the old armchair on the veranda. Ramen assured us he had allayed his brother's suspicions tactfully, but we were all quite uneasy after that.

And now Ratan must have informed the CRP company posted in the adjoining district. How he knew about our plans was beyond us, but then Ramen always talked too much. He must have let something slip. As it is, we had not been able to cover much ground—it is not easy, I realized, to slaughter a human being. A goat or a chicken is different—it does not wail in your language while being butchered. We had not foreseen this. I almost lost my nerve a few times, and once, I felt quite frightened when I saw a group of people emerging from their huts at the far end of the village. But they were only trying to make a run for it and probably went and hid themselves in the jungles nearby. I had pushed on. But now this!

Pratap had assured us that he had had a discreet word with OC Kalita who had recently been transferred to our police station. He said the officer-in-charge had assured him he would not interfere.

'Just signal when you are done, I will bring my men. I have to be seen as doing something, no? Heh heh!'

After all, Kalita was also Axamiyā, and hated the immigrants as much as we did. The CRP, on the other hand, had no sense of affinity with us; they only followed the Central Government's diktat.

But where did they come from? They were camping a few villages away and Ratan must have informed them well in time if they were already there.

There was nothing to be done now but flee. We all ran. We made our way through the dead bodies, and jumped over other bodies that would probably have been better off dead, and ran. We scattered in different directions as we had already planned to do after our task was completed.

Even as I ran, I thought I saw Ramen picking up something from among the dead bodies. I could not stop to find out what.

Suddenly, my red Naga shawl got stuck on something as I turned in the direction of Na Pam. I bent down to release it by brushing away what could have been a small hand or a fallen branch. I did not have time to think about it. I also heard police sirens. Naturally, Kalita could not be caught doing nothing when the CRP arrived.

I crossed the bamboo thickets praying that I would not trip and fall, or worse, get bitten by a sleeping snake on whose tail I might inadvertently step. When I was clear of it, I made for the first house I saw. It was Sharma saar's. He had been our Axamiyā teacher in college, and we had always made fun of him in class. At least till we realized he had just moved to our village. My father would have skinned me alive if saar had ever complained about my behaviour in class. After that, we merely sometimes let the air out of the tires in his bicycle so that he would have to pull it the entire five-kilometer stretch home.

I knew saar was the nervous kind. We often made fun of the way he looked so alarmed every time someone so much as greeted him with a 'namaskar, saar' a little louder than usual. Inside the classroom though, he was a different person, confident in his learning and passionate about his texts to the extent that sometimes, even I found myself drawn into the history of our Xankari culture or recollecting some of the *jotua thas* he explicated lucidly—so much so that I would sometimes use these traditonal Axamiyā sayings at headquarters and get teased for being a 'kobiraj'. Then, when his lecture was over and the boys started asking silly questions, he would go red in the face, his lips would quiver, and he would quickly leave the classroom.

Knowing him to be the kind of person who was easily startled and who jumped at every little thing, I knew that if I knocked on his door now, he might have a heart attack. But I had no option, the sirens were drawing nearer. I prayed that *baideu*, at least, would have the courage to come to the door. She had taught us history and was rather stern, quite unlike her husband. We all used to be afraid of her in college.

I wiped my face as clean as I could on my shawl, hid the *da* under it, and guided by the faint moonlight, quietly made my way to the kitchen door at the back. I winced as I stepped on the *kharikajai* planted along the drawing room wall just below the window. *Baideu* would definitely not like it when she saw the plight of her flowers in the morning. But I had no way of avoiding them as I groped my way along the sidewalls of the house in the darkness.

Our League had called for a black-out that day in the entire state as a protest against the state government's inability to throw out the immigrants, and the Central Government's apathetic stand towards the entire issue. Everyone was bound to follow our diktat or their houses would be stoned and windows broken. We had imposed the last few calls successfully and I was glad to see that no one in Na Pam dared leave their lights on anymore during black-outs.

There was only a faint yellow glow visible along the outline of the kitchen window that had newspapers pasted on the panes from inside. As I had hoped, saar and *baideu* had not gone to bed yet. Nobody did sleep very well these days.

I imagined they must be sitting at the kitchen table keeping vigil. And then of course, the sirens were also sounding quite loud by now. As I approached the kitchen door, I could hear soft murmurs. I knocked softly on the door. The murmurs suddenly died out, the yellow glow faded.

'Saar, *baideu,* it's me—Prabin. Can you please open the door?'

When I heard no movement inside, I knocked again, a little louder. This time, *baideu* opened the door a crack. Saar stood behind her. I could see the fear on her face, and although in the near darkness I could not see his, I imagined it would be contorted in terror.

'*Bopa*, son, what are you doing here at this time? And what is all this commotion about? What is happening?'

'There was a raid at our League office. Somebody misinformed the police that we were hiding arms there. Can I come in and stay here for the night till this is over?'

I could sense them stiffen, and I knew that they did not believe a word of what I had said. With his hand clutching the kitchen door for support, Sharma saar was visibly shaking, so was the door itself. But *baideu* was a sensible woman. She knew it would be no good trying to turn me away. I blessed my quick thinking about the arms story. Now even if they did not believe my story, they would not dare raise an alarm.

Baideu let me in and quickly shut the door again. The sounds of the sirens faded. I felt safe in the glow of the dimmed oil lamp. As I stood in the middle of the kitchen floor now, unsure of what to do next, there was an uneasy silence for a short while. *Baideu* broke it.

'You will eat something?' she asked rather stiffly.

'No, *baideu*.'

'You will sleep?' she asked again.

'If you can spare a room...'

She said I could sleep in the drawing room. Their two children, Majoni and Moina, were asleep in the other room and she did not want them woken up.

'That will do fine. I can sleep on the drawing room floor. I will leave before Majoni and Moina are up. No need to see me out in the morning. I will leave before dawn.' I knew I was rambling. A combination of relief at finding someplace to hide and rest for the night and tiredness from the night's labour was catching up. I fell asleep immediately as I lay down on the drawing room carpet.

I do not think saar and *baideu* slept that night. I could not be sure. I was woken up by *baideu*'s screams.

'Moina, Majoni! Don't touch that!'

It was light outside. I had overslept. I sat up quickly. I saw that Moina was holding my *da* in his hands. Majoni was picking at the dried blood on it with her tiny fingers. The Naga shawl I had used to wrap the *da* in lay at their feet, thick with dried blood. Saar stood in the doorway, afraid to come in. And *baideu* was pushing him out of her way, screaming and lunging at the children, and finally, snatching the *da* from them. She then ran at me with it, brandishing it menacingly.

'You dare come into my house with blood all over you. You dare expose my children to your murderous ideology. Murderer!'

Last night, in the darkness, they must not have seen anything, but now that it was daybreak, I imagined they could probably see my hair matted in blood, my clothes caked in it. The children, however, did not seem perturbed. Moina's bright eyes were turned towards me in fascination and Majoni was now picking the blood stuck in her fingernails with rapt attention.

'Labhita, don't! Let him go. He will go away. Go *bopa*, go, please leave. We will not tell anyone you were here. Just don't come back. Please!'

Sharma saar seemed to have finally found his voice. But he pleaded with me from the doorway, and still did not enter the room. A few steps from me, *baideu* suddenly broke down. She crumpled on to the floor and began to weep and wail.

Saar was still trembling and *baideu* still on the floor when I packed the *da* once again in my shawl and left. And I was also trembling when I drowned both shawl and *da* in the river on my way home. I figured I could not go home looking like this, and took a dip in the river myself and saw the waters around me turn red.

We met at headquarters that evening. All of us looked like we had slept through the day. At least, I knew I had. At first, we could not think of anything to say to each other. Then Pratap said, 'At least we are all safe.'

'Yes,' we all murmured.

'It was close though,' Pulakes began.

'I will deal with Ratan, *salla,* just wait!' Ramen was suddenly animated.

'At least it was not an utter waste,' he said and emptied out the contents of his pockets on the table that we were seated around at the center of the room. We saw a few bangles and finger rings and earrings, some made of gold and some of silver.

I could not understand why the jewellery was there on the table.

Then, I jumped.

One earring still had the lobe attached to it.

I Don't Love Sam

It was not easy not loving Sam. For twelve years, I thought I was in love with him before I could finally admit to myself that I had always loved Sam the notion, and never, possibly, the person. He was everything that was beyond reach, everything forbidden. Insisting on loving him was my way of rebelling against the norms of my family, the education system that tried to mould my character and the society that governed my choices. But I was not to know all this until much later. And when I did, my rebellion began to seem quite pointless.

When I first saw Sam I was twelve. I was the brightest student in class, he was the son of the school gardener. In our residential school run by Catholic nuns, it was drilled into us that even looking at boys was a sinful act. The patron saint of our school was a young girl who had killed herself rather than be 'kissed' forcibly by a boy—or so we were told euphemistically. We could not wear short skirts: they had to cover our legs down to our calves. We could not wear short socks: they had to cover our feet up to our calves. We had to wear pristine white shirts, preferably with full sleeves. Hair tied in red ribbons, nails short and clean, no flashy jewellery.

'They might as well make us wear those bulky habits,' some girls often complained. But it was not just the dress that we found so constraining. We had very little contact with the outside world and our everyday lives were governed by a strict routine that was supposed to keep our minds away from sinful thoughts. We were trained to see God and his divine message in everything: even our extra-curricular activities revolved around God Almighty. From our singing classes to dramatics to work experience to physical education, everything was aimed at equipping us to find the morality and divinity within us.

Being at the age that we were, attaining godliness was, of course, not among the priorities in life for most girls. Besides, most were extremely resentful of all the restraints imposed upon them by the school. But our parents had deemed such discipline necessary for the development of our characters and had thus sent us to this school. Girls, their middle-class background dictated, should learn virtuous living and moral values. The Catholic nuns could drill that into us. Being educated in an English medium school would also give us an edge in life and ensure we got good secure jobs, or at least married good guys with secure, stable jobs.

Our school was among the best in Assam. Its reputation was such that even parents with die-hard rightist leanings conveniently suspended their inherent mistrust of Christian institutions and were willing to make huge donations to get their girls enrolled. And it is true that we were given an excellent education: our school alumni consisted of very prominent citizens. It was every parent's dream to see their girls scale the same heights.

My parents had also sent me there with the same intentions. They were happy when I started scoring the highest grades in class and also excelling in most extra-curricular activities. I loved singing and dramatics and no school play was complete without me. I also wrote the occasional poetry which I would send home to my father. A writer himself, it would make my father very proud to send his daughter's poetry to the local magazines and newspapers and see it published. Every time one of my poems got published, I would find a special mention in the morning assembly in Mother Superior's address. I was the teachers' pet, never getting into any trouble, always a stickler for rules. In other words, I invariably came through as the perfect conformist, unlike most of my classmates.

Quite a few of my classmates, who regularly broke curfew to read adult magazines under torchlight at night or earned repeated reprimands for wearing their socks rolled down, did not like me much. They could never believe that even I found the school rules constraining, or that even I wished I could sometimes roll up the sleeves of my shirt, or not have to brush my shoes every morning. I did not always want to sing hymns in singing class or play the virtuous husband in the school play. I rather enjoyed playing Faustus and selling my soul to the devil the one time that we performed Marlowe.

But I never rebelled outwardly like the other girls. My rebellions were always silent—like when I wrote about carnal love in some of my poetry. If the Salesian Sisters had read my poems before they were published, they would have burnt them—or me—at the stake. But once the poems had been published in reputed journals, they could do very little but praise me for the good publicity I gave to the school in the outside world. My biggest rebellion, however, was falling in love with Sam.

I saw Sam for the first time one day when I was returning to the dorm after a particularly long practice session for a school play. I rather fancy it was *Doctor Faustus* because it would fit in perfectly with the theme of selling my soul to the devil, but I cannot really be sure now, so many years down the line. He and his father were not allowed out in the school grounds till teaching hours were over and the girls had returned to the dorm for lunch. They worked in the garden for a few hours thereafter, till it was time for the girls to come out for their evening stroll led by one of the Sisters, forming a straight line, hands behind their backs. They could not be talking among themselves or they would find themselves faced with the most ignominious command of all, 'Finger on your lips!'

Sister Theresa, who had always been particularly fond of me, had held me back that day after everybody else had left. She was walking me back to the dorm still discussing some lines, when I nearly stumbled and fell over Sam who was weeding one of the flower beds along the way. After we exchanged apologies, Sister Theresa introduced me to Sam and his father. As we continued on our way to the dorm, she told me how they had come to live on the school grounds.

During the ethnic riots in Barbari, where Bodo and Adivasi villagers had attacked each other, Sam's family had lost everything, including the mother and two sisters. With very little government aid forthcoming to rehabilitate the people affected by the riots, a few Catholic organizations had come forward to help them financially and spiritually as they struggled with their grief, trauma and loss. A few years later, the government-run relief camps were shut down and the displaced people were forced to go out looking for alternative places to stay. The Adivasis were the worst affected and most of them had lost their land. Being agriculturalists, they did not possess any other livelihood skills to sustain them economically. Some of them approached the Catholic organizations for help. They opted to convert to Christianity so that they could get employment in Christian organizations and institutions.

Shyamkanu Murmu's father offered his son up for conversion while he himself adamantly retained the faith of his ancestors. And after Shyamkanu became Sam, father and son came to stay in our school and work as gardeners. When the Sisters saw that Sam was very bright, they began to take a keen interest in his education as well. Now Sister Theresa and a few other nuns gave him regular lessons and Sam had impressed them all with his sharp mind and quick intellect. They had high hopes of training him for priesthood and sending him back someday among his people to preach the word of Christ.

As Sister Theresa narrated all this to me, I do not mind admitting that my first reaction was a feeling of being privileged. Nobody in school ever treated any of the girls as adult enough to tell them about the harsher realities of life. And here was this old nun who did not mind shaking me up a little with the tales of such horrors. Did she really think I was mature enough to handle the truth? At the same time, I was also seized by a sense of self-pity at how little I knew about the outside world. There was so much going on out there, so many people were suffering, so many upheavals were taking place every day, but I was ensconced in a protective cocoon and had no access to any of it. None of it affected me, whereas people like Sam had seen so much and been through so much, their life experiences must have enriched them in a way that I could never hope to be. Immediately as I thought this, however, I suddenly remembered the pain that such experiences must have brought with them—the loss of family, of home and hearth, of kith and kin, of everything familiar, and things held dear. And I felt ashamed of my own thoughts.

For a long time afterwards, I kept trying to bump into Sam once again, intending to somehow make up for my initial insensitive reaction to his story. After many abortive attempts, I approached Sister Theresa herself with a bold proposal. I went up to her and honestly admitted that I could not help thinking about what she had told me about Sam. I told her I wanted to help him in some way and perhaps I could assist her during the lessons she gave him?

'Silly child!' Sister Theresa laughed benignly. 'Give him lessons? He is two classes ahead of you already, and could give *you* lessons if you wanted.'

'But he looks so small, Sister.'

'He does, doesn't he? That's what hunger and deprivation does to you, child. They were never well off to begin with, and then the riots took away whatever little they did have.

He is a handsome boy, although so dark like all his people. Let him stay here for another year and he will grow big and strong and then you will not recognize him at all,' she laughed again.

Indeed, as Sister Theresa had predicted, Sam's bony structure soon filled up with strong muscles and his dark skin was stretched tight against his frame. I used to watch him sometimes on the sly from the dorm window as he worked in the garden, and fancied I could see his sweat gleaming in the sun, his skin shining. At night I would dream of running my hands over his glistening body, his tongue licking my skin in return, and wake up sweating and shaking from guilty passion. During the day, whenever I met him, I would fervently hope that his sharp eyes could not penetrate my soul and uncover my secret fantasies.

I would meet him quite often now, thanks to Sister Theresa who had, after all, arranged for me to give him Axamiyā and Hindi lessons, neither of which the nuns could manage. Our regular Axamiyā and Hindi teachers could not spare the extra time required and these were the two languages Sam had to learn if he was to function in society outside of the school. After the initial few lessons, it was no longer me teaching Sam but the two of us learning together, sitting under the big Krishnasura tree in the school yard most afternoons. But neither of us complained. We had become fast friends.

Sam was a great storyteller, telling me about his old life in the village, his old school which only had half walls and no benches, and during lessons, stray cattle walked in and out of the classrooms that had no doors. We would laugh then and I would wonder how Sam could be so matter of fact about it all. I thought I would have felt bitter and deprived if I had to study in such a school. Then I would contrast the closed environment of our school with the wall-less, door-less school Sam had gone to, and wonder at the disparity.

Sometimes Sam also told me about his mother who was killed in the riots, how she would hum old, nearly forgotten folksongs under her breath as she went about sweeping the front yard or making frescoes of mud and cow dung on the walls of their tiny hut. She would watch over his father as he got drunk every evening with friends and neighbours who would come to taste the best *haria* in the village, the one she brewed painstakingly at home. They never had plenty but she always managed to keep her three children well fed and happy. Then his eyes would burn with hatred towards an unseen enemy when he spoke of his sisters whose dead bodies were recovered in the jungle two days after their village had been burnt down. At those times, I would feel like I was looking into his soul, uncovering the real person he was.

Sam was not the school gardener's son, Sam was not the future priest the nuns were hoping to see him grow into. Sam did not belong to the Church which had taken him in and had such high hopes from him. He was also not the man who came to me now almost every night in my dreams and fuelled my latent desires. He did not belong to me either and although I knew this with a certainty, I vowed to love him forever, like I loved him then and for all the rest of the four years he lived in our school. Even when he left to complete his higher secondary studies in Guwahati and I had to stay back in school without him for two years, I continued to love him silently, rebelling silently.

I was rebelling against dear kind Sister Theresa who

always said I was the most compassionate girl she had ever seen, and how Christian it was of me to care about the less fortunate. I never thought Sam was less fortunate, for me he was always richer for his life experiences. I was also rebelling against my parents who would never deem a poor village boy, non-Axamiyā at that, deserving of my affections in any way. I always thought I was the poorer person, having nothing to offer but the false middle-class values I had grown up with and a shallow morality that had no place in real life.

No, Sam did not belong there under that Krishnasura tree. He belonged back in his village, among his people. One day, I knew he would go back.

A thousand different emotions were churning inside me as I dialled the mobile number scribbled on my grimy notebook. *Shyamkanu Murmu (Sam) 9864074837*. The look he gave me the last time I saw him, two years back, should have deterred me from making this call. I knew what he thought of me—and it wasn't flattering. Why then was I calling him again now? What did I have to prove to him? Why did I have to prove anything to him at all anyway?

The Sam I knew had turned into somebody else when I met him in Guwahati after I left school to join B Baruah College for my BA. Once out of the protective school environment, I learnt some very harsh lessons. One was that I was nobody special; there were hundreds, if not thousands, of other talented and intelligent people everywhere, many of them much more talented and intelligent than I could ever be. Which is why I did not get into Cotton College where all the bright students go. Sam though had easily got admission there: he was exceptional when I knew him in school and spent so many afternoons in his company, he continued to be exceptional in the two years that I barely saw him except for a few brief visits he paid his father and the nuns while school was still in session for us.

In those two years, I would write to him regularly, tell him silly little details about my daily life, send him cuttings of my published poems, ask him for his opinion, beg him to tell me about his life in the hostel, the city, the outside world. His replies, whenever they came, were very brief and never warm towards me. They would, however, be full of invective against the 'oppressors' and the 'bourgeoisie', and about the need for the rise of the 'proletariat'. His passion for communist literature fuelled mine and I would spend hours reading Marx and Engels in the school library. Very little else was available in the limited collection in our library but by the time I left school and joined college, I learnt that Sam had moved on from the communist ideology and was now talking of self-determination and ethnic identity and nationalism and the need for retribalization. He spoke passionately about his ancestors who had been brought to Assam from Chota Nagpur by the British to work in the tea gardens or cultivate the wastelands. They had stayed back since they first arrived in the nineteenth century and had embraced the local culture and language. But they were never accepted here, and they would always remain the pariahs unless they stood up for themselves.

So Sam renounced Christianity, much to the disappointment of the nuns who, nonetheless, continued to shelter his father in the school. He also changed back his name to Shyamkanu Murmu through an affidavit in the Gauhati High Court.

'They cannot make us forget our roots forever. Such conspiracies never work for too long. We have been fools, but now we know that if we are to survive, we have to reclaim our lost identity,' he would declare between puffs of post-coital cigarettes, for we had now taken to sleeping together often in his dingy hostel room, away from the watchful eyes of the nuns and my parents' moral injunctions.

'Yes, but what's changing your name got to do with it?' I would ask.

'The personal is political, Jonali. The personal is political,' he would announce gravely, expelling more smoke through the lips that had tugged at my breasts not long ago.

And once again, I found myself trying to keep up with him. I would never miss a single Political Science class and looked forward to studying Sociology for my MA: our college did not offer Sociology at the BA level. What I could not look forward to, however, was to ever belong to Sam or for him to ever belong to me. Once, when I started talking about a future together with him, his whole body stiffened. I could feel his muscles bunch up under my cheek as I lay with my head on his shoulder. He never held me after sex, I never wanted to let go. He withdrew into another world, I into his.

'We do not have a future together, Jonali. I thought I had made that clear from the very beginning.'

He never had, but I could not open my mouth to correct him just then, or I'd break down.

'We both enjoy each other's company and that's all we

can share. I have never made any false promises to you, so you cannot hold anything against me.'

True, he had never promised anything. But didn't having sex mean anything? Didn't holding another person, sleeping together, talking together, being together amount to anything? Didn't nine years of friendship and closeness mean anything, lead anywhere?

Apparently not for Sam, and as I valiantly swallowed my pride and my hurt, I remembered the resolve I had made so many years ago in school to love him no matter what. I had accepted then that I could not have him to myself; I reconciled myself again, now, to the fact that there were certain things that were greater than the individual: like one's ethnicity, one's own people, and one's ideology. I wanted desperately to reason with Sam that our being together should make no difference to his identity and his ideology; that I could be his partner in his fight to get his people their due because I empathized; and that if we ever got married it would be the perfect politics born out of the union of two individuals from the two communities at the extreme ends of the ethnic hierarchy.

'It would set a precedent,' I had said desperately on the eve of my departure to Delhi where my parents were sending me to study Sociology as I had wished, and to keep me away from Sam as they thought fit, after they discovered I was still seeing him.

That was when he had given me a look of utter contempt. 'You and your people are all the enemy,' he had said and walked away.

And now, two years later, I was back, nursing a deep wound, and a void inside me that nothing could fill: not a new place, not new friends, nor new ideas, or new preoccupations. In retrospect now, I realize that it was never a void, but a Sam-sized hurt that I was carrying around with me everywhere. Because I made space for the pain he gave me, nothing and nobody else had been able to enter my life. Not the awkward elder brother of my D School classmate who came to visit me at the hostel with a whole crate of mangoes when his sister mentioned I loved the fruit, nor the passion to prepare for the GRE exams so I could go to the US for my PhD as my parents wanted me to. I guess I held on to this pain because, somewhere, I knew I had lost Sam: if I could not have him, I could at least hold on to the hurt he gave me.

I ran into an old college mate of Sam's a few days after returning from Delhi and he told me that Sam had joined politics soon after college. That came as no surprise to me. He said that for a while, he had been the rising star in the Adivasi community and it had been predicted that he would go far in state politics. Once again, that was something I had always expected. The college mate had followed Sam's career through the newspapers where he would be mentioned quite often.

'I ran into Sam about a year ago and saved his number in my mobile. You can have it, although I am not sure it is still functional. I have never tried to contact him on it. For you, that's the least I can do,' he said meaningfully, because he had known how much in love I had been with Sam.

When I first dialled the number that he gave me and nobody picked up the phone at the other end, I was almost relieved. But, instinctively, I redialled, and the voice that answered was unmistakably Sam's. He sounded drunk and it was 11 o' clock in the morning. Or maybe he had been sleeping, I thought as I said, 'Sam?'

'Jonali?!' He sounded surprised and bemused.

'Yes, it's me. I am back. Where are you?'

'You know, I really don't know.' More bemusement.

'What do you mean you don't know, Sam?' I realized I had come out more strongly than I intended.

'I was at a party last night...Our local legislator, you know...Great man...He personally invited me. I am his right-hand man. He cannot win elections without me. He has promised me a ticket next time around. Then I will also be a minister. Then everybody will know what this Shyamkanu Murmu is all about! You, your nuns and your people, and everybody else who always looked down upon me, pitied me, took me in so that you could feel great about yourselves. You will know...'

He was still blubbering on when I hung up.

I set the phone down on the table beside me, leaned back on my parents' living room couch, and closed my eyes. Slowly, I felt the pain I was holding on to for the last two years flow out of me. I realised there was an emptiness inside me, a lightweighted-ness. I could have felt regret for a boy who had everything despite losing so much; or pity for a man who had everything by the sound of it, but had lost himself, perhaps forever. I felt nothing. After twelve years of being consumed by Sam, of having every thought, every feeling, every pain revolve around him, I suddenly found myself feeling free; free to say to myself, and to anyone who cared to know, that I did not love Sam.

Not anymore.

Colours

Blue

Mur ee antar khani xagarar dare nila bedanare...

—Debakanta Baruah

This my heart is blue like the sea, with pain. I always thought I could feel this pain, this intense agony, deep down in my heart. I always feared this pain will be with me till the end, refusing to go away, which is why I decided I should do something about it, maybe leave it all and go away, go far far away, from my parents, from all acquaintances, and from the familiar places that had shaped my life and given me this pain.

I was born in Guwahati, a city I called home but where I never really felt at home. Many like my parents had come to this city from mofussil towns and villages to build a new life, and in the process, had started imparting to the city, just as the city had imparted to them, hypocritical middle-class values. These were also the values that have always repulsed me so much, and instilled in me the desire to run away, be in some other place, assume some other persona. I always blamed these values for my parents' lack of courage: the kind of courage one needs to be able to match up to one's ambitions. So, of course, they capped their ambition at a stable job with a secure income, and perhaps it *was* a lot for them to achieve in a new city with a new way of life, and, true, they *were* willing to do anything to achieve that ambition—but only if it could be done without any kind of confrontation with anybody.

My mother was the more ambitious of the two; my father just sort of went along. He came from a very poor family that did not have enough agricultural land to be shared among the five sons, of whom my father was the fourth. So, he had to come to the city to look for a job. My mother's father was a fourth-grade officer in the district magistrate's office, and he earned enough—very little of it by way of government salary, of course—to keep his sizeable family of six daughters and two sons in relative comfort. She moved to the city when she married my father.

At first, my mother was appalled by how little my father made at his job as an officer of the State Bank. What was more, he seemed content with the job and his salary. My mother had enough ambition for the two of them, and as such, forced him to take all the qualifying exams that would get him promoted through the ranks, sitting up nights to ensure that he did the same, till he became a branch manager with a decent salary and the scope to earn some more on the side. After that, she used the influence of one of her father's acquaintances to join a government school as a subject teacher, and turned her attention to making something out of me. I was admitted to one of the three elite English medium schools in Guwahati at the time, a school that had a Catholic management and was, therefore, sure to instill the kind of discipline she thought would take me far in life.

I was not an extremely bright student but good enough to keep her ambitions for me alive. Although I came to know early in life that she planned for me to be a doctor—because doctors are never without a job and make lots of money besides—I always wanted to be a writer. Even when I grew up and got to know that writers, especially in Assam, make almost nothing from their writings, I thought my parents had made enough for me to live on for the rest of my life—and then some—so that I could easily indulge myself and my passion for poetry and literature, which I had developed while still in school.

But my mother would have none of that and she made me sit for the medical entrance test, which I cleared in the second attempt, thus falling behind my classmates and losing what little I had by way of friends and companions. My mother persisted, however, and when I did get through, I was so bad at studying medicine that I kept falling behind in class more and more. I finally emerged an MBBS doctor—taking two extra years to earn my degree—and in the absence of any desire to pursue a specialization, started looking around for a job, any job, that would take me away from Guwahati and my parents and the ignominy of being the only one among my contemporaries who was not yet a specialist, gainfully employed, and married.

Then, one day, I got a call from the Kalguri Tea Estate authorities for an interview, and when I reached the tea garden and saw the colonial bungalow set aside for the doctor and took a walk among the tea bushes for the first time in my life, I knew that I had to get this job and come live here.

I did not care that in a tea estate, the frequently changing doctors are mostly retained for ornamental purposes, with the local compounder being the one the labourers all came to for his reassuringly familiar, high-handed, bumbling system of medication that he had developed through years of trial and error. After all, I never did perceive of myself as a qualified enough doctor, having been always behind in class. Now I became only too eager to come to Kalguri to unlearn all that I had learnt.

For the first time in my life, on the night before the interview at the plantation guest house where I was given accommodation, I felt a kind of peace trying to make its way into my heart, nudging at the precious pain I had nurtured all these years. As I stood in the huge lawn and bathed in naked moonlight, I knew if I came here, I would have all the time in the world to indulge my passion for literature, and to read and write to my heart's content. As I looked out at the rows and rows of tea shrubs in front of me, I could feel every novel, every poem, every word I had read about lives hitherto unknown to me come alive and call out to me, entice me, irresistibly pull at every molecule that constituted my being.

I did not waste any time setting out for Kalguri when the appointment letter reached me a few weeks later. My mother had always said she would not let me go so far away to Delhi or Bangalore to study like many of my friends and cousins had done, because she could never be sure whether I was applying myself enough, but I knew it was really because she could not bear to have me slip out of her control. However, I was almost twenty-eight now, and could not bear to be near her anymore. I needed to break away. Even if it meant being only 400 kilometers away from her and lying to her that I wanted the effortless tea estate job so that I could prepare for my postgraduate exams and would be back in time for the exams in six months, I managed to get her to agree in the end. The fact that the tea company was paying me a very handsome salary must also have had something to do with her acquiescence.

The six-hour journey to Kalguri may not have seemed momentous to others who were also making it; after all, there were many people who travelled back home to Guwahati every weekend from what they thought of as punishment postings at Kalguri village, which had grown up around the tea plantation, or in the town of Barbari nearby. For me, though, it was a remarkable journey, because for the first time I felt free, on my own, and on my way to shedding the agonizing blue that had housed itself in me all these years so tenaciously, and it suddenly seemed to me, in hindsight, so melodramatically.

And strangely, as the bus began crawling its way out of Guwahati, I saw the evening sun reflected in the waters of the vast Brahmaputra, and the fantastic blue of the sea—that neither I nor the poet Debakanta had ever seen—seemed already to be shedding its sadness. Instead, seeping into my soul now was the satiny blue of the Brahmaputra tinged with the crimson of the setting sun.

Black

Tourou thakiba pare janu bhem
Naharani baganar koli mem...

—Pranab Barman

Can you too be so arrogant/Black memsahib of Naharani garden? I had come to Kalguri wondering whether it would turn out to be my Naharani, where I would find my black memsahib and a tragic love affair. I had been in love once, earlier, at medical college, but she had left me because of my lack of ambition as she perceived it. How would she know that I did have a lot of ambitions; only they weren't the kind she or my mother would understand?

My ambitions were not limited to jobs or money; they had more to do with finding people, discovering places, and getting rid of all that blue. During my initial days at Kalguri, every time I saw a pair of muscular black calves below the undulating folds of a grimy sari walking away from me, I would wonder if she could have been my Chameli memsahib, and I—though not a white man—could be George Baker, shedding sweet tears of sorrow, while in the background Bhupen Hazarika sang his heart-wrenching ode to tragic, doomed love, 'O *Bidexi Bandhu*...'

But I did not fall in love in Kalguri, and all the black memsahibs gradually lost the romantic sheen I had draped them in. They became everyday people like their brothers or fathers or lovers or uncles, all of whom warmed up to me enough to soon start offering me their *haria* to drink and allowing me to participate in their evenings of *jhumur* dance once in a while. Alcohol had been taboo in our house, but now, having left behind the Hindu traditional universe I had been confined to, I got more and more attached to the drink. The more I drank, the more I rose in their estimation as somebody who was 'not like the rest of them.'

Often, I would get too drunk to walk back to my bungalow on my own and a few of them would carry me and put me in bed. They felt good that the doctor sahib was fraternizing with them, no doctor at the tea garden had ever done that before. And I felt good that they were accepting me more and more into their lives, and often congratulated myself that I could shed my ingrained elitist education and upbringing to mingle with the workers and labourers.

I stopped going back to Guwahati every weekend like I initially did under pressure from my mother. I also stopped calling as often as she would have me call her. My mother kept threatening to come down and stay with me, but I kept putting her off. My father made the appropriate amount of fuss, then gave up. My mother persisted, but I learned that it was easier to handle her long-distance and mastered the art within a short time. All in all, my life at Kalguri was going quite well. I was leading the kind of idyllic idle life I had always dreamed was necessary for any kind of literary pursuit, whether reading or writing.

The tea plantation had an excellent library, which had been built up over the years by the erstwhile white masters of the estate, and I was catching up with all the reading I had missed out on in the years wasted at medical school. When I wanted my dose of Axamiyā literature, all I had to do was send one of my orderlies, Dambaru, on his cycle to the village headmaster Praphulla Narzary's house and I could have the learned man's handpicked selection of the literary masters.

Whenever I was in the village, I would visit him and discuss all that I had read with him, over cups of steaming tea or glassfuls of *jou* that his daughter, Deepti, had brewed. I would often cycle back to my bungalow late in the night, despite Narzary saar's repeated warnings about gunmen on the prowl at that time. Every time I was late, he would apologize for not having kept track of the time, and plead with me to stay back at his house for the night rather than get shot by the militants or the army, whoever happened to be around. But the *jou* would have made me fearless, and happy like I had never been before, and I would ignore his pleas. Besides, as I always reasoned with him, it would not look nice if I stayed the night given that he had a young daughter at home, and nobody else.

Sometimes, when I returned late at night from my trips to the village, which gradually became more and more frequent, I would find a potful of *haria* left at my door. No doubt by Dambaru who followed me around like a little lost black puppy most of the day, and at night missed me if I did not come to their basti to drink. Then I would drink some more of the *haria* or risk offending Dambaru and go off to sleep.

No matter what time I awoke, Dambaru would be ready with my breakfast. After breakfast, I would go off to the hospital. I would sit there as long as it took for the compounder, Biswas da, to have his paranoia come back and feel threatened by my presence and say kindly to me: 'You must be tired, saar, why don't you leave? I can handle it here.'

Sometimes, the manager's wife, who was nothing less than a queen in the tea estate, would summon me to administer her insulin and I would spend a couple of hours talking to her about nothing of any consequence. And as soon as I could leave, I would return to my books or cycle down to the village or walk around to the labour basti. Once in a while, the manager or the assistant manager would invite me to come along with them to the Planters' Club where the management of about ten tea gardens in a radius of two hundred kilometers would meet whenever they felt they needed the company of their peers instead of the illiterate, uncivilized labourers whom they were forced to deal with day in and day out. I would accept the invitations at reasonable intervals but come back sickened to my stomach by all the flirtatious advances of the planters' wives.

All in all, I was packing in more experiences during my stay here than I had ever absorbed in my whole pathetic life before. And I should have been able to write like I had always planned to, but I was too busy soaking it all in to find time to reflect and recollect. I was not complaining, however, and was perfectly happy with the way things were—till one day, I killed Dambaru.

Yellow

Tumi mouk bhal pale
Sarimuthi halodhiya xuta kini dim...

—Jiban Narah

If you love me, I shall buy you four lengths of yellow thread. These lines always now remind me of Deepti wearing her yellow *dakhana,* sitting at the loom, looking up and smiling at me every time I pushed aside the horizontal bamboo poles on their gate and walked into their yard.

How was I to know that Dambaru was in love with Deepti? How was I to know that Deepti—the college-going daughter of the village headmaster—could be in love with a boy from the tea tribes, an uneducated, quiet mild-mannered boy, whom I sent to her house so often, at all odd hours to collect books for me?

Surely it was because of me that this could happen but other than Narzary saar, nobody in Kalguri village was willing to allow that fate also could have had a role to play in the development of this socially unacceptable relationship. When the lovers were caught holding hands and strolling along the river bank one day, it became a matter for consideration by the village elders; and though the Bodo community to which Narzary saar and Deepti belonged was largely detribalized now, it did still retain a characteristically tribal distrust of outsiders. No Bodo could marry a *harsha* or outsider.

And what is more, Dambaru's tribe was not even indigenous: his grandparents had come from somewhere on the Indian mainland as bonded labourers to work in the tea plantations and had settled here. It was to free their indigenous land from the occupation of outsiders that many Bodo youths had taken up weapons today, and if it should be known that a girl from their village was involved with a tea tribal, the entire village would be in trouble.

I was present at the meeting and I could sense the fear as well as the anger. But because Narzary saar was well respected, they let me off with a small fine. Dambaru, however, was not so fortunate. He was found killed just outside the tea garden one morning. Nobody could or would say who did it. But everybody began to keep their valuables packed in small pouches, ready to abandon the village at the first signs of trouble. Able-bodied men from the village started staying up nights on sentry duty. I was forbidden by the plantation authorities to go to the village, and I could also not go to the labour basti anymore, because even though they did not openly accuse me of anything, I could sense that they felt betrayed.

Meanwhile, the news of Dambaru's death had made it to the newspaper as it had followed closely on the heels of ethnic clashes between Bodos and tea tribes in the adjoining district. The media predicted that ethnic riots were imminent in the Kalguri area also. My mother read the news and decided that I should come back immediately. Two years was long enough to have wasted in a remote tea plantation and according to her, it was time I got out of this mess and came home to take stock of my life.

I told her I could not come. For the first time in my life, I was straight with my mother. I told her that now more than ever, I could not and would not abandon the people who meant more to me than anybody else had ever done in my entire life. The city meant nothing to me, and though I did not directly tell her this, I am sure she also understood what I left unsaid—that she herself meant very little to me. She, who stood for all that I hated: a limited life, constricting values, and a self-centered universe.

As I stood my ground for the first time in my life, I suddenly realized that I myself had epitomized the things that I had hated all my life. What had I done for the garden labourers who had welcomed me into their lives so uninhibitedly? I had taken their affection for granted and not even rendered them the service for which the garden management had hired me in the first place. On the contrary, I had jeopardized their very existence.

It was not as though I was not aware of the tensions prevalent between the two communities—even though remote, news does travel to Kalguri. And there had been ethnic clashes in the neighbouring districts only a month ago. Yet, I had sent Dambaru to the Bodo village over and over again, in order to satiate my own lust for literature. I had been blind to the growing affection between him and Deepti because I had not paid attention to either of them. I was so engrossed in my discovery of Narzary saar's treasure trove of knowledge that I had become insensitive to the boy who ungrudgingly acted as my go-between and the girl who quietly looked after my comfort while I was engaged with her father.

Had I only acknowledged their existence and made an effort to know them as persons, I could perhaps have gauged the growing involvement between them, and helped them before things got out of hand. Who knows? And now I will never know because Dambaru is dead and Deepti cannot even mourn his death because if she showed any signs of mourning, the villagers would ostracize her father. As it is, they blamed her and Narzary saar for the imminent attack on their village, although nobody said it openly.

The attack came one night. There were people with bows and arrows and some with guns. Two Bodo villages in the area were razed and twenty people killed. The same night, five tea tribe villages were also set on fire, and fifty people made to stand in a line and riddled with bullets. Dambaru's basti was inside the plantation and the management had received prior information about the date of attack. So they had shut all entry points into the estate and tightened security. Word was that they even paid the militants not to deplete their labour force. Cheap labour was hard to find and any untoward incident inside the plantation meant losses amounting to hundreds of thousands of rupees every day. So Dambaru's basti was safe, but Deepti's village was razed to the ground. And Deepti had disappeared. The survivors had to go live in a relief camp twenty kilometers away in Kalibheta.

Two days later, when the plantation management allowed me to take the official jeep, I went to the relief camp. Narzary saar sat under a tree and would not talk to me. The other villagers met me coldly and told me nobody knew anything about Deepti.

As I was coming back to the estate, my driver stopped on the roadside to take a piss. There was a mustard field there, and it was all yellow with mustard blossoms. I thought I could see clotted black blood splattered over the yellow.

Red, Green, Grey

Issa hoi tar hatar ranga patakakhan
Jui huwar agate
Tat jen xeujiya xutare buta basi aki dim
Puwatit jak pata uranta maral...

—Geeta Goswami

I want to snatch the red flag he carries/Before it flares up/And weave into it with green thread/A motif of a flock of maral/Spreading their wings in the morning light. Between file shots of the red and green flag of their organization, the local news channel was showing pictures of Deepti in handcuffs. That was when I discovered that she had joined the militants after that night.

She told me later that she was carried away by the attackers, who dumped her in a mustard field not far away from the village. From there, she was picked up by a group of men who did not seem to belong to either community, but were armed with guns. They had raped her, repeatedly, and dropped her off near the army camp at Barbari and she had crawled her way to a nearby village, which luckily for her, turned out to be a Bodo village. There she was nursed back to health and indoctrinated in the militant ideology.

Because she was well educated, she rose quickly through the ranks and they used her to write press releases and demand notes and to communicate with the media. She told me all this when I went to meet her at the Guwahati Central Jail five years later.

After watching the news, I spent a sleepless night, wondering if I should go and see her. In the end I decided I should. It took me some amount of maneuvering with the jail officials to be allowed to meet her, but I managed in the end and I am glad that I did.

She also seemed genuinely glad to see me. She told me how she had been away taking military training in the hills of Karbi Anglong when her father died. She had gone to see him when she came back two years after the carnage, but he was no more. He had died in the relief camp alone, abandoned, away from home.

When I asked her why she joined the militants when everyone knew that they were the ones who had killed Dambaru, she did not reply. Instead, she asked me what I had been doing with my life.

I told her how I had taken the easy way out and escaped to the city. My mother had said nothing, but I could sense her triumph when I sat for the Assam Public Service examinations, qualified in my first attempt, and asked my father for money to pay for a position at the Guwahati Medical College. I had been leading a quiet life since then, and next month, I was getting married to a girl who my parents had decided would be good for me.

She said she was very happy for me. I asked her if she intended to surrender now that the government paid generous rehabilitation packages to surrendered militants.

'You mean get co-opted into the system, like you? Yeah, I might,' she said.

This Is How We Lived

It is nothing, really. It is just the story of our lives, has been for years now, and we see no end to it. It is what happens to us—so many of us. It is just a kind of trade, routine at that. They buy us and they sell us, and because we want to live, we do not resist. We give in to their lust because most of the time, our lust for life proves to be more compelling. But sometimes, I feel that maybe, for them, it is not even really lust, you know. Maybe it is just an outlet, a way of getting it out of their systems. Maybe if they did not rape us, they would instead fire at us.

They often do that in any case, and indiscriminately too, like that Punjabi soldier from the nearby army camp did in our village five years ago and killed two children—brother and sister—walking home from school. The parents were later berated for letting their children walk around unchaperoned while there was a war going on.

The army officer who had come to 'pay his respects' to the family after the incident ended up shouting, red-faced, at the wailing parents: '*Kaise mata-pita ho?* What kind of parents are you, allowing your children to run around in the streets like this? Don't you know the terrorists are everywhere? We are here to protect you—but we cannot do our job properly if you do not cooperate! As it is, they killed your children, see—the terrorists killed your children—it was their bullets that killed them. Do you understand? *Samjhe?*'

The Public Relations Officer standing next to him was wincing inwardly. So much for building personal relations with these people and trying to win their hearts and minds and turn them against the rebels!

Although they did not understand much Hindi, in the face of the officer's tirade, the parents started wailing louder. What could they say that would convince anybody otherwise? Mangal and his gang—the village loafers who played carrom all day under the *thinthlang* tree in the village square—had seen it all and had told them about the drunken soldier who did it before their very eyes. The soldiers would stop and play with them once in a while during their patrols through the surrounding villages and chat with them, and talk to them about games and sports and their families and friends back home. An uneasy camaraderie—if one could call it camaraderie—had developed between the two unlikely groups of people, one that would prove to have been illusory that day.

Like other days, that day also, the group of loafers had been playing carrom when the patrol had come by. For some reason though, a few of the soldiers had been drunk—one more so. He had to be propped up by his colleagues every now and then. Even before their vehicle came to a stop, he had started shouting obscenities at the boys, and not in the usual friendly manner either. This had put Mangal and the others on alert, but even so, they were taken totally by surprise and were filled with fear when they saw him raise his gun and send a volley of mock fire all around him.

'*Jajajajajajajaja*,' he had shouted in imitation of gunfire while turning round and round, taking aim at everything and everybody in sight, including his colleagues who watched him and laughed. After going at it for a while, he suddenly stopped. He had seen the two unfortunate children running down the street toward the square, the first ones to be rushing out of school at the end of the day as their mother had promised to cook special pork for them that day.

And then just as suddenly, the firing was not pretend anymore, but real. Real live bullets shot out of the gun and the two children dropped to the ground. The other children who were following them not very far behind, started screaming and running back to the school house. Mangal and his friends just stood there, petrified. The soldiers got quickly into action and rounded up their colleague and rushed away.

A few papers tried to report the truth, and people read them too and were angry. But even though Mangal and one of our teachers spoke out, they could not get many other eyewitness accounts to substantiate their claims. A few of the other newspapers, mostly the mainstream 'national' papers that reported the incident in about sixty words, did not even bother to change the language of the press release handed out to them by the army PRO—that the children had got caught in the crossfire during an encounter of the Indian Army personnel with 'hardcore terrorists'.

Our village stopped producing hardcore 'terrorists'—as they like to call them—after Simang died three years ago. Till then, we had really believed in the revolution, and thought it would do us good. Simang was among the brightest students of our school, and we all had great hopes of his going on to become the first graduate from our village. He matriculated from our school and completed his higher secondary studies from Barbari college with a second-class degree. Seeing that he had to walk twenty-five kilometers to and from college every day, the teachers of our school had all raised money to buy him a bicycle. The day we handed it to him, he cried. We told him we were giving it to him only on the condition that he would complete his studies and do 'something' for his village and his people.

The headmaster's voice shook with emotion when he spoke to Simang from the dais during the school meet we organized to hand over the cycle to him: 'You are our hope. This village as much as this school needs you to complete your education and come back to teach the younger generation the same values of community and culture that we inculcated in you. We are old now, our days are numbered. But you are the future. You will have to serve the cause of our people.'

Simang did go on to serve the cause of our people all right, but not in the way we had thought. He joined the rebels while still in his first year of graduation studies, and we heard from him later that he had gone to many foreign countries to be trained in the use of arms and weapons with which to fight the mighty Indian Army. He was our local hero for many years thereafter, as were the six other young men, also like him, who had given up individual prospects to fight for the future of our community. For years afterwards, concepts like sovereignty and self-rule, identity and self-hood flooded our conversations and took over our minds. We were dazzled by the promise of a future where we would not be looked down upon, where we would be our own rulers, where we would have the rights over our own land, practice our own culture, enrich our own language, live lives of prosperity—in short, a golden future. And naturally, the young boys who were taking on the powerful Indian state in order to acquire that future for us were our heroes.

It was only when the boys started dying and the army started their war on our hearts and minds and we saw no change in our sorry lots that we began to see the futility of this golden dream. One by one, the boys from our area who had joined the rebels started to get killed, either in real or staged encounters. Simang's killing was staged to make it look like he was trying to flee from custody, when the fact was that not only he, but his two brothers who were farmers, not rebels, had all been tortured to death. After this, nobody from our village joined the rebels. The loafers alone swaggered around, posing as rebels and collecting money from people in the marketplace. 'Protection money' they called it; they had finally found an occupation other than playing carrom. The carrom playing had anyway stopped after the killing of the children.

In fact, after Simang and his brothers were killed, many things changed in our village. The loafers, as I already said, became 'self-employed'; the army started entering deeper and deeper into our community life, holding cultural shows in our villages, celebrating our festivals with us, and organizing free health camps for our people, so much so that even if they killed our boys now, there would be some among us who would refuse to believe that those killed might have been innocent. And then there was the complication posed by Mathuram's daughter.

Mathuram's daughter was picked up by a few soldiers one day on her way to school: she was going to sit for her matriculation examination. She walked into a house full of mourners three days later, nothing Bodo about her except her looks. She was wearing a salwar-kameez instead of a *dokhona*, there was sindoor on her forehead and a mangalsutra dangled from her neck; her husband, a Hindu soldier from north India, was with her. They had been married by the priest at the small temple inside the army camp the day before. They sought the blessings of Mathuram and his wife, were granted it by the bewildered couple, and were gone two days later to the soldier's home in a small village in Uttar Pradesh. Even though marrying a *harsha* is a serious offence in our society and calls for a village council to levy fines and determine the offerings to be made to the gods, in this case, everybody was too fearful to attempt anything or show any contempt for the outsider.

Mathuram's daughter wrote regularly to her parents—I would read out her letters to them—about how happy she was in her new home, how her in-laws were so pleased that she was learning their language and customs so fast, and finally, in the latest one, how she was with the soldier's child. Her happiness confused us. It was easy to hate and fear the army as a whole for all the atrocities that they committed, for all our people that they killed, for standing in the way of our golden future. But then there was this one soldier from Uttar Pradesh, a *harsha,* who loved one of our girls so much, he married her and took her home where she was now expecting his child. Her letters told us every day what a good man he was, how he brought so many presents for her every time he came back home from his distant postings. How now do we hate them all, now that we knew they were not all the same?

Already, the dream that we were given of a golden future had begun to be replaced by a banal reality of death and gore, the understanding that life would go on if we just started accepting everything passively, without complaint. When Simang and his brothers were killed, we had taken out a silent protest march and tried to draw attention to such fake encounter killings. We also wanted to hire a bus and go to Dispur to hold a demonstration in front of the State Secretariat. But Simang's old parents stopped us.

'What good will it do? Our sons are not coming back to us. Let the sons of the other people in the village live.'

That was our cue, and we started accepting whatever came our way with a kind of fatalism that was more ennui than stoicism. A few of our political leaders and human rights activists did stop by, but we were not the epicenter of the insurgent movement—ours was a small village, not in a Bodo majority area, surrounded by villages inhabited by innumerable other communities, and we had produced only seven rebels in nearly a decade. When they saw that we also lacked the will to fight back, they decided to leave us alone. In any case, there was no other major incident involving the armed forces or the insurgents in our village for a few years afterwards. Mathuram's daughter shook us out of our ennui for a while, but soon, we learnt to live with that riddle also.

That was when Bogi bai came to live among us—when nothing seemed to be happening at all in our village, not even a skirmish, just a few local goons creating a fuss now and then; while everywhere in Assam bombs were exploding, planted either by the insurgents or by the security forces posing as insurgents; and people were being killed, arrested and maimed for the crimes they had committed against the system or to cover up the crimes the system had committed against them; and politicians and activists were shouting hoarse about real or inflated injustices against our community; while we just lived on from day to day.

She was the granddaughter of Shibram daroga, the only policeman our village had produced during the British Raj. When we were small, we would huddle around the *thinthlang* tree in the village square every evening and hear the stories our elders narrated about days past and places far away. One of their favourites was the story of Shibram daroga, the brightest boy in the entire village, who was orphaned at a young age. The day after his uncle—who had brought him up like his own son—got married to a young girl almost his age, Shibram left home to join the police force. Within a week, he had married and left to train for his new position in Guwahati. From there he took postings in Dhaka, Alipore, back to Guwahati, then Meerut, and so many other places the names of which our elders could not even pronounce. They said he once saved the life of a white man while he was posted in Dhaka and that facilitated his quick promotion to the post of a daroga. In any case, as befitted a respected official of the British Raj, Shibram daroga never returned to his village in his lifetime, neither to meet his relatives nor to claim his ancestral land. Once in a while though, through messengers, he would send money to his aunt. The uncle had died a couple of years after the marriage, leaving the young woman with a daughter and ten bighas of land, half of which would have gone to Shibram daroga if he had returned to claim it.

But he did not, and neither did his son, Pradip Musahary, who grew up and continued to live far away in Meerut where his father had built a house after retirement. He married a *harsha* from Himachal but she was not with him when he visited our village once, many years ago while I was still in college, to attend the wedding of his father's cousin's son. I remember how we stood and gawked at him from a distance and laughed as he awkwardly attempted to speak with his great aunt in Bodo. Finally, he gave up and spoke to her in broken Axamiyā—Shibram daroga must have insisted on his speaking in Axamiyā at home rather than in Bodo, because he thought that if his son ever had to return to Assam, he would have to speak the language of the majority.

Tribal languages did not seem at the time to have any future in Assam and he had seen the disdain with which the Axamiyā Hindus of the nearby village had treated the tribal people from his village. It was only after he became daroga and was posted in Guwahati once again that he had been allowed into the houses of the Axamiyā officers and aristocrats. On his first posting as a new recruit to the police force, fresh from the village, he would have to sit outside on people's verandas, and if offered tea, would have to wash his teacup before leaving. He settled in Meerut because he did not want his only son to face this kind of treatment—at least this far away, nobody knew the difference between a Bodo and an Axamiyā, and both were equally alien and savage to them. And yet, Assam was home and it was possible that he hoped that someday, his son would return to the land of his ancestors. His son did not return, though, after that one visit. His granddaughter did. And she never left, till she died.

Bogi bai was not her real name, but we called her by that name because she was so fair, she glowed. Many people in the village initially thought she was a daini, a witch, and wanted to kill her, or she would put a curse on our crops and on our children. It took a lot of effort on our part to dissuade them and to get them to believe she was only human. It took some more effort to get them to accept her presence in the village without complaint. And finally, after a year or so, almost none of us could remember a time when Bogi bai was not living in our village or was not a part of our everyday lives, strange though her ways had always been and continued to be.

She had only asked her cousins for one katha land—the rest, she said, they could continue cultivating as they had always done. Then surprising us all, she built a mud and thatch house on her land: all the rich people in our village preferred to build concrete houses with cement and bricks, at times brought all the way from Guwahati. Then she began planting vegetables and fruits around the house in her small piece of land. Her cousins gave her a portion of the paddy they produced and for the rest, she lived off her garden. Pulses, pork, chicken and fish were available every evening in the *bwjai* market that was organized exclusively by the women of our village and the villages nearby. But though she paid for her purchases, she almost never remembered to pick them up from the market at the end of the day, when she returned home after having spent the afternoon and evening talking to the women who came to the market to sell silkworms and dried chicken skin, and all types of green leaves and vegetables, and pork and fish and *jou.* Almost every day, she would sit with the women in the *bwjai* market and drink as much of the *jou* as the rest of them—sometimes more—and make them tell her all the stories of their lives.

'*De de,*' the women would say to each other when they

saw her drunk from the *jou,* 'She is Bodo after all, although she speaks like a *harsha.*'

Bogi bai was only just picking up the language, and polishing it during her daily conversations with these women, and with the other people of the village.

Often, it would be late in the evening when she would walk back to her house clutching a fat red diary where she would have made notes during the day, recorded anecdotes, and entered little nuggets of information that she had picked up. She told us she was writing a book—a novel—for which she was living among us and talking to us about our lives; she visited every house in the village in the course of her first year and always talked to everybody about their lives. Once when she came to the school to meet the teachers and speak to some of them, I asked her why she said so little about her own life.

'There is very little to tell, *abo*. I had a rich father, loving mother, comfortable upbringing, good education, and I lacked nothing; nothing except a sense of belonging. I did not belong even to my own husband after I got married. When we got divorced, I decided to come back and search for my roots. So here I am, although a little late in life, trying to understand who I am, where I came from. But I hope that at least I can also tell the world a little bit of my story through my book, once I have actually grasped it myself.'

This was the longest she had ever spoken about her 'other life', as she jokingly called it many times, trying to evade the probing questions of the inquisitive villagers.

'Let us not talk about my other life, please,' she would say. 'I am here to talk about your lives, and write about you all.'

And since they were flattered that they would be included in a book that the whole world would read—it was to be in English, and many of the villagers could not even write in Bodo—they would not pursue it any further, at least till the next time somebody spoke about it again. After she told me about her divorce in school that day, I passed the word around that nobody should trouble her with questions about her past life, since I sensed it was not a very happy place for her. They had some regard for me—I was school principal now—and so they did not pursue the matter with her anymore, although they did pester me for details for a while. I had none, and had to cook up some, which I did thinking it was all for a good cause. I eventually managed to de-mystify her for the people of the village, though I wasn't any closer to solving her mystery for myself. Slowly the questions subsided, and Bogi bai became one of us and she remained one of us till she died.

Often, when she was returning home from her daily interviews, it would be dark. We all warned her not to walk back alone. After all, these were bad times, and even though we had created a bubble around us that no amount of mayhem could burst—or so we led ourselves to believe—we did know deep down that anything could happen at any time. There was the army camp just a few miles away from the village, there were the rebels who paid intermittent visits—to keep an eye on things—and most dangerously, there were the surrendered and pseudo rebels who knew nobody could touch them: they either had no scruples, in which case holding them accountable for their misdeeds would make no difference, or they were blessed by the state machinery and could, thus, not be held accountable for anything. True, we had taught ourselves to live with all of this, or maybe despite all of this. But it was also true that every once in a while, one of the households would find their daughter or wife or niece or mother gone for one night or two. And when they returned, they would be seen bathing themselves in the river over and over and over again. Everybody knew, but nobody wanted to say anything, because it was more important to go on living a lie than die facing the truth.

Ever since the army camp was set up in the nearby village fifteen years ago, every woman, every girl for miles around, knew instinctively to underplay her femininity, and never to be out alone, especially after dark. Nobody thought of it as something unnatural; it had become a mundane part of our everyday life; this was how we lived. There was no point in attracting undue attention. They would eventually spot you anyway, and summon you to the camp. But Bogi bai did not pay heed to our warnings. I sometimes suspected she must have felt that because she was educated and well off and could speak Hindi in the same accent as the North Indian soldiers, she would never be manhandled by them. But all she said was, 'Who would try to harm me? If I am in any trouble on my way back, somebody will come to help me. Everybody in the village respects me, knows me.'

Of course nobody from our village would want to harm her, but Gandrai was not from our village. He was from Kajalgaon and he would sell his mother if they paid him two hundred rupees. Usually, he got paid between fifty to a hundred rupees for the local girls, depending on how pretty they were, or how drunk the soldiers were. But Bogi bai was a lady, extremely fair, and educated. She had to fetch a higher price.

So Gandrai sold Bogi bai to some soldiers from the camp and one night they came and picked her up from her house. The next morning, some men from our village found her dead under the *thinthlang* tree, her *dakhana* lying on the ground near her. This was the first time any of our women had been killed. Usually, they were kept for a night or two and then let go. But Bogi bai was dead. Maybe she had resisted; maybe the soldiers who bought her off Gandrai were in a particularly bad mood. After all, they also have a hard life. Our boys who fight them know that we their people have to finally side with them no matter what—that's what community and kinship ties are for; but these soldiers do not even have the illusion of fighting for a cause. They face death every day for a pittance, to send home a few thousand rupees every month. Out of that, if they spent fifty or hundred rupees on buying the bodies of our women, perhaps it does not seem like a bad bargain to them. Perhaps it is like a routine trade, an outlet for their frustrations, and the pressures of functioning under tough conditions in a conflict zone.

We do not want to be killed, and so we make these excuses for them. For ourselves, we say nothing, just wash ourselves ten times, maybe a hundred, and try to forget it happened, till it happens a second time, or a third. But if it happens even once, we get used to it, and inured to the ignominy. We have started looking at it less as an affront to our dignity and more as a price we have to pay for living in comparative peace in the midst of a mini war. We did not start the war, somebody else did. Many people are paying for it with their lives; the least we can do is be thankful we are alive. This time however, it was different. This time somebody died; this time Bogi bai died.

It seems she had had some influential friends in her other life with whom she had been in touch occasionally. When they got to know, they came to our village and did a spot survey and went back to Guwahati and submitted a citizens' report and demanded that an inquiry commission be set up. The newspapers also were full of the news for the next few days. The inquiry commission was set up within a month, and every once in a while, we heard that there was some noise being created about 'the case' either in Guwahati or in Delhi, but both places were too far away from us. A couple of times, a few investigators came to question us if we knew who was behind 'the incident'. We all knew, of course, but nobody said anything because once the outsiders left, we would still have to live here. And indeed, after the last of the investigating teams left, we heard nothing about 'the case' anymore.

Bogi bai had been one of us. Her parents had died some time ago, and she had never mentioned any family left in Meerut. In any case, nobody did come forward to claim her; only some friends had come and they had done their bit to find her killers, of course. But we were her family, her kin. So when her body came back from the autopsy, and they had taken as many samples as they needed to satisfy the press and the activists and the politicians and her influential friends that they were doing their best to identify the culprits, we did with her what we do to ourselves after coming back from the camp. We washed her body carefully, once, twice, three times, I don't know how many times, till we were sure that she was clean. And then, we cremated her.

'Write Romola'

I was choking, gagging. But he was pushing it further down my throat. I could feel the bile rising up from my stomach, but it found no outlet and kept churning around at the base of my throat where the tip had lodged itself. I thought, not for the first time since I married this man, that I was going to black out. But because this was not the first time, I also knew how it would go. He would continue to shove, I would continue to choke and just as I was blacking out, a part of my brain would come to my rescue: the part that opened and closed the sluice gate of all my memories, lived and unlived—of other lives, half lives, soul connections and interrelations with people sometimes met, sometimes not yet met. And I would escape to that world, oblivious of my present. For as long as it took, I would go live in that world so that I could survive this. Then, when he had withdrawn and flopped down on the bed, I would make my way to the bathroom, clear out the contents of my throat, flush, rinse, brush, floss, mouthwash, trying not to return, but knowing that as soon as I opened that bathroom door and stepped into the bedroom, I would be closing the door to my other world behind me.

Today in that world, I met Romola, yet again.

Romola had raised me. She was herself a little girl, barely ten years old, when she came to stay with us. The third daughter of distant relatives from my father's ancestral village, her mother had sent her to our house because they couldn't afford to feed another mouth.

'I have taught her to cook and clean. She is a very smart girl. Living in the city will do her good. Just take her away from her father, bapu,' her mother had pleaded with my father and he had brought her home.

My mother was very unhappy that my father had brought home such a small girl—and Romola looked even smaller for her age. 'I already have three children to look after, and then there's all of your relatives from the village who drop in whenever they feel like. Now you've brought another child home! Who's going to look after her? The children go to school while I'm away at college. Where will I leave this girl?'

I was the youngest of us three and had started going to school way ahead of other children because that was the only way my mother could save her job at the college and bring home her much-needed salary. If she didn't work, we couldn't go to the private Catholic schools that my father had flatly announced he couldn't afford. He had to divide his salary equally between the city home and the village home. After all, his elder brother's sons were also his responsibility since his brother was an opium addict and did little to provide for his wife and children. So when it was time for my eldest brother to go to school and my mother wanted to give him the best schooling available in our city, she had to take up a teaching job herself. By that time, my second brother was also almost of school age, and I was on my way. I do not know now—and I cannot ever know—how my mother managed with us three children, born so close together, and feeding and taking care of a bunch of relatives and village people who were in and out of the house all the time, while working as a full-time college teacher. But I do remember her being bitter most of the time; and I seem to recall her and my father fighting a lot: over money, over relatives, over us. Even way back then, crying into my pillow, I remember telling myself, over and over again: 'Marriage is not for me. I don't want *this*, ever!'

I do not remember the fights over Romola though, maybe because she very quickly became an extension of our family and remained so for the next twelve years. But Romola herself told me, years later, that there had been many in the first few weeks of her coming to Guwahati. The woman had a knack for remembering things all of us very often forgot. Like how I used to sit on the floor and flay my legs, refusing to go to school, and how she would cajole me into wearing my uniform and tell me stories while walking me there. Or how my elder brothers would pull at her pigtail and make her cry, and when she complained, my mother would berate her saying she was a big girl and should know better than to fight with the boys.

'But then *baideu* would feel bad, *jano, Ma-dhon.*' Only Romola ever called me *Ma-dhon*. 'And her way of saying sorry was to give me one extra biscuit for tea, and none to Baputi and Xoru.'

In those days, chocolates and biscuits were a luxury for us, what with so little money to go around, and if my mother had given her one extra biscuit for tea and none to my brothers, it had to mean something.

Growing up, Romola would often recount these stories, and somewhere along the line, I stopped questioning which of those memories were my own and which were borrowed from her. It was as if she was the keeper of my memories, and whenever I needed to return to those days, all I had to do was talk to her. She would hold my hand and lead me, a little girl again, down that path. Sometimes, my mind would rebel and go back alone, like in those terrifying dreams of school exams I was entirely unprepared for. But even in those dreams, Romola would turn up at the school gates in her bright floral frock. She would be waiting for me, as she had always done, hands on her hips, two umbrellas dangling from either side, ready to take me home.

Throughout my twelve years in school, it was always Romola at the gate. As we made our way back home, I would recount to her what we did in class that day. She knew all my rhymes and school songs by heart. Once, my mother heard her reciting the 'Hail Mary' in her sleep. When I sat down to do my homework, she would bring out the notebook and pencil my father had given her and doodle along. Later, she always said she was grateful to me for teaching her how to read and write. That way, her scheming half-brothers in the village could not wheedle away her family's share of her father's land.

'They asked me for my thumb impression on some papers, but when I said I could sign my name, they got scared and ran away with the papers,' she announced triumphantly on coming back from one of her rare visits home alone. A few days later, the half-brothers turned up at our house and my mother read the documents carefully before allowing Romola to sign her name on them. Now that her father was no more, the property had been divided equally between the two families from the two wives he had kept. He had been found dead one morning, bullet wound to the head, in a bamboo grove some distance from the army camp outside the village. Nobody seemed surprised.

Romola had not gone home for his cremation and shraddha. She had never spoken about her father, and we were not too interested anyway. But once when we were in the village, I had overheard Baputi da trying to convince my father to turn her father over to the police. My father, of course, said nothing.

'He cannot go around doing this to all his daughters, no?' Baputi da had yelled as he walked out of the house towards the pond in the backyard. I knew something terrible had happened—again—but dared not ask. I'd never heard my cool college-going brother's voice break with so much emotion.

After her father died, Romola suddenly developed a new fondness for her family, even her extended family of stepmother and half-brothers. She would often go visit them despite my mother's constant worries about a young girl travelling alone when the police-military were everywhere. 'If I die, I'll die,' she would say with pursed lips.

'I'm not worried that you will die, you silly girl. I'm worried that you will have to live with a fate much worse.

You think your family will take care of you then? We are the ones who will have to live with that burden!' my mother would snap.

She would go anyway, and when she returned, safely every time, the two of them would not speak to each other for days.

She would also borrow money from my parents—who were better off now that their respective colleges had been provincialized and salaries raised—to pay her brothers to cultivate her piece of land. Then, every January, during the Magh Bihu celebrations, she would go home and bring back some of the harvest. Her brothers would sell most of it. She would take her share of the money, whatever her brothers paid her, and repay my parents. The rest, she would deposit in her cooperative bank account.

My brothers would often tease Romola now, saying she was a landowner. 'Romola Zamindar', they would call her and she would chase them around the yard, shouting at them to stop calling her names, and we would all have great fun.

❧

The fun stopped when all at once, or so it seemed to me, everybody started leaving home. My mother said she was tired of pacing up and down the driveway every evening till she saw the last of her children turn the corner towards the house. 'We have to send them away,' she announced one day.

My father said no—and for a long time thereafter, they fought again, a lot.

'I don't want my children falling for the glamour of the revolution,' she screamed. 'Baputi is drawing machine guns everywhere these days! I saw his notebook! How long do you think before he actually picks up one?'

'Kalita did not send his son away, nor did Bhagawati. And their sons are not gunmen. Why do we have to send them away?' my father countered. 'Cotton College is still the best,' he proclaimed. 'And I have no money.'

In the end, my mother borrowed money from her brothers. A year apart, my brothers left home to stay in hostels far away: Baputi da went to Delhi and Xoru da to Nagpur for their higher studies. And Romola left to get married. I lost my brothers *and* my companion within a couple of years. Baputi da and Xoru da would still come back home from time to time, but Romola was gone forever. She came back only once, about three years later, just when I was myself leaving home for Delhi. She had heard from somebody in the village that I was leaving and wanted to say goodbye. She came the day before I boarded the train to Delhi.

Either the intervening years had robbed our relationship of its warmth, or I was too involved in myself and the new future that awaited me, away from home, but I found I could not connect to Romola the same way. We made perfunctory gestures of familiarity, said stilted goodbyes, and she left the same day.

'*Ma-dhon*, remember me,' was all she said as she turned to leave.

I was in Delhi for nearly eight years thereafter, studying, working, getting married. I would come back home sometimes, but more often than not, it was my parents who would visit me. Sometimes, Baputi da and Xoru da would fly down to Delhi to join them and we would feel like a family again. Albeit, a family that had a very tenuous connection with what used to be home. I blamed it on the violence. There was always a bomb blast, a blockade or a riot to justify our staying away. My brothers did not make excuses; they simply made their homes elsewhere. Xoru da married and lived in Mumbai while Baputi da eventually left for California. Their lives in Assam were a thing of the past. But I could not ease off the baggage called 'home' so easily.

After graduation, I joined a prominent news magazine as a cub reporter. Before long, I had proved my writing skills to my editors. They realized I wasn't the 'hard news' type. I would do best at the features desk, they said, and made me cover the cultural and literary scene in Delhi. I enjoyed that a lot: meeting celebrity artists and authors, attending cultural events and book releases, going to parties and drinking wine while discussing the latest trends in the arts and in literature, pretending nothing else mattered.

But soon, certain incidents started shaking me out of my torpor. Like when I introduced myself to a favourite author as being from the Northeast, and she exclaimed, 'Oh, but you look normal, like us!' Or when I found a colleague from Mizoram crying on the stairway behind the office building: a male colleague, a mainland Indian, had called her a slut because she wore 'tight-fitting' clothes. She was sobbing, 'You Northeast women are all sluts,' he said. Apparently, we didn't know what was Indian because we wore tight-fitting Western clothes. And so I wrote a series of articles on what it meant to be a Northeasterner—a person from the peripheral states of Assam, Nagaland, Manipur, Mizoram, Meghalaya, Arunachal, Sikkim, Tripura—on mainland India; on what made us different and yet, the same; on how we were part and parcel of the 'unity in diversity' ethos of India.

The more I wrote about feeling alienated in my own country, the more I started following events and developments back home. Then, one day, there were serial bomb blasts in my city and my parents narrowly escaped getting killed. I wrote a fiery, extremely passionate, personal essay the next day on how I understood why 'our boys' had taken up the gun to fight the Indian State, why we were still outsiders in a country we had embraced as our own, and why, despite all of that, bombing and gunning down people was not the answer: 'we' needed to try harder to gain acceptance, just as 'they' needed to become more inclusive. When it was published, I received many congratulatory phone calls from friends and media colleagues. One call came from my husband-to-be. A senior correspondent with a leading news daily, he swept me off my feet when we met after a few friendly phone conversations. Soon, we were married. And just when it was taking off, my writing career ended.

I did not realize, of course, that that was what was happening. The initial years of marriage were wonderful. It was as if I was living in a dream where my husband would turn up home in the middle of a work day with a bunch of flowers: 'Just to say I love you!' And to have sex. It almost started seeming like working from home wasn't too bad after all.

At first, I had been a little apprehensive about giving up

my full-time media job, but my husband had convinced me that that was not my scene.

'You are a writer,' he said. 'The newsroom is not where you will thrive. I will work hard enough for the two of us, bring home the money. You just sit at home and write. I want my wife to write a bestseller, not have to worry about fending off drunk testosterone-driven power-hungry men who objectify women.'

Like most other women in the media world, I too had had some unsavoury experiences with men who thought they controlled the world (especially its women) just because they controlled the way people saw it. I had told my husband about one particularly unsavoury man and he had threatened to beat him up for me. What woman wouldn't be smitten by such protectiveness?

I gave up my job and followed my dream: I became a freelancer, writing what I wanted, for whom I wanted. Trouble was, I started writing less now that I had more time to myself. Without really realizing it, I was spending most of my time setting up the new house, looking after its daily management, preparing the husband for work, cooking his favourite dishes, cleaning. Then one day, dusting one of the bookshelves, I found an old folder with my early writings in it—including that much-acclaimed essay. As I squatted on the floor, reading the essay, I could not believe I was the same person whose byline was printed on it.

'Who have I become?' I asked my husband at the dinner table that night, wanting some reassurance.

'You are still the same scintillating writer,' he reassured me.

'I don't feel like a writer any more, I only think like a wife,' I persisted.

'Is that so bad?'

Suddenly, he was not focusing on his dinner plate, but was staring at me.

'No, of course not!' I rushed to reassure him in turn. 'You know I love being your wife! But I don't want to forget who I am.'

'I'm not asking you to,' he said as he abruptly left the dinner table.

I never brought up my writing with him again, but he did.

If I said I didn't like a dress he bought me, he'd say, 'Of course I don't have the refined taste of a writer!'

One morning I told him his late-night games on TV disturbed my sleep. He snapped, 'I'm not cerebral like you, I need my mindless entertainment.' And he smashed the TV with his cricket bat. Sometimes, he would take his anger out on other household things like the dishes or my flower pots; more and more frequently though, he started taking it out on me.

Seeing my parents fighting, I had never wanted to get married. But I did. And so I got what I deserved for forgetting my childhood resolve. At least my parents had never hit each other, or broken things—they had bickered. I learnt now to make that distinction. But it didn't help me. I was already broken.

It did not always feel like an unmitigated disaster, though. There were times, after all, when I saw glimpses of the man whom I had fallen in love with. Like when he cooked special meals for me and our weekend guests, or bought me new books. Or when he introduced me to people at parties as 'the best writer I've read (and I've read many)'. But no matter how brightly I smiled or how many glasses of wine I downed, I never felt happy again.

There were times when I wanted to talk to somebody, tell them how sad I was. I could not. I had married this man out of love and I couldn't admit to anyone that I had misjudged him. I could not tell my parents: they would be devastated. I could not talk to my brothers: they were thousands of miles away and, besides, they had their own families and their own problems. I did not have any friends in Delhi, not really, not since I had stopped going out anymore for fear of being found out. And my childhood companion, my Romola, had vanished from my life.

The more I retreated into myself, the more I found myself remembering Romola, wondering where she was, what she was doing. I remembered she had married a shopkeeper from her village. Her mother had found the match for her and had come to our house to seek my mother's permission to take her back home. My mother had many questions to ask about the boy before she was convinced that he would be a good match for our Romola. I had been too busy in the kitchen teasing Romola to pay any attention to the conversation the two mothers were having, deciding her life for her. Sometimes now, I wished I had listened in, I wished I had a clue. I wished I had talked to her the last time we had met.

But wishes aren't horses to take you back in time. And

even if they were, I did not think I was left with the energy to drive them there. Not until, one day, I found myself being presented with the opportunity to do so.

In one of the media parties my husband sometimes dragged me to, dressing me up in clothes that he picked for me, I met an editor I had worked with in my first (and only) job. On discovering that I was not doing anything productive with my life, she gently chided my husband, 'You should let her go out more, meet more people, write more. She had so much promise!'

'I keep telling her that, pushing her out of the house. But she's such a homebody,' he protested as he pulled me closer into the circle of his arms, planting a soft kiss at the top of my head.

'Aw, that's so sweet of you!' she said, and offered me an assignment. My husband could not say no.

The magazine was looking for somebody to write about women in the Northeast who have lived through the insurgency, about their experiences of and contributions to the conflict. She remembered the pieces I had written all those years ago, and wanted me to write again. My husband said he was delighted for me.

For the first time in many years, I felt something like excitement building up inside me. I felt like I had won some kind of a battle with my husband. It did not matter that I had not fought the battle at all; that I had no fight left in me. For the first time in many years, I had a field assignment. As a bonus, I got to go home to my parents to work on it.

My husband drew up an itinerary for me to follow, a list of places to go to, and contacts to get in touch with.

'They're all excellent journalists, good friends of mine. You should meet them and get your information,' he said and cautioned, 'Don't get too adventurous. I confront danger every day in my investigations, so I know where that can lead you.'

As I said goodbye to him at the airport, my head felt lighter than it had in years. But my heart was heavy with the nagging thought that maybe I was being set up to fail, yet again.

I spent the first few days at home, being pampered by my parents. Now that they had both retired, they lived comfortably on their pensions. My father's elder brother had died a few years back. His nephews were all grown up and did not need him anymore. So when I visited them, my father seemed more present and my mother less perturbed about things. Both of them appeared to have mellowed down in their relationship. Not that they had grown fond of each other or something, but at the very least, they had developed a mutual tolerance. Each had learnt to give the other their space. Sleeping in my old bed at night, I kept wondering if my husband and I would ever reach that stage, if he would ever give me my space.

He had started demanding a child now, but we were having trouble conceiving. The gynaecologist had said I should learn to de-stress.

'You have such a loving, caring husband. And you lack nothing. Yet, your husband says you overthink everything. Why take unnecessary stress and poison your body?'

Maybe this trip would help, I thought. Maybe a child would help.

But when I went looking for Romola on that trip, ignoring the itinerary my husband had drawn up for me, I learnt that having children does not help. It certainly did not help Romola. She had started giving birth right after marriage. Within the first two and a half years of marriage she had had three children. They had all died. They said she killed them.

When I told my father I wanted to start working on my story by interviewing women in his village, he was overjoyed. Although not quite at the heart of the insurgent movement, the village, like all villages in Assam, had witnessed insurgency. It was as good a case study as any. So we drove down there and I interviewed all the relatives and other villagers who had gathered at the ancestral house to meet with me. Romola was not among them though. As we were leaving, I casually asked somebody where she was. They told me she was dead.

We drove back to the city in silence. My father slept most of the way, I stared out of the window. But when I reached home, I could not take it anymore.

'Why didn't either of you tell me she was dead?' I shouted at my parents.

'It would have needlessly upset you,' they said. They were in agreement on this one.

'When? How? Tell me!' I demanded.

My mother hardly kept in touch with my father's side of the family, nor did she go to the village much. But my father took off as often as he felt like, and every time he did, he visited Romola. So he knew the story better and he told me. He told me how she had found out, not long after their marriage, that her husband was an informant for the insurgents. He also apparently allowed them to store their weapons in his shop. What had Romola more worried, though, was that he was, at the same time, passing on information to the Indian Army.

'Our boys come at night. They bring wild pigs and hens with bullet holes in them, and I have to cook those for them. Sometimes in my dreams, I stumble upon his dead body riddled with bullets,' she had whispered to my father.

'The others,' she had said, 'the ones who have licenses for their guns, they come at all hours. They keep looking at me. I don't like their looks.'

Romola said her in-laws kept pressuring her to have more children. Her first three children had died because nobody would allow her to take them to the civil hospital ten kilometers away when they had diarrhea soon after birth.

'There's something in the water here, but if I say that, they tell me not to behave like a wealthy lady from the city.'

My father said he strongly suspected Romola did not want any more dead children and that was why, after the death of the first three, she had had three miscarriages.

'If you want your children to live, you must love them. She's no mother, she is a witch,' her in-laws would tell the villagers. 'One after the other her children died, and see how she struts around like a memsahib!'

Whenever she asked her husband to intervene, he would beat her. Once, they had to take her to the civil hospital and stitch her up. My father had come to know later, and had tried to convince her to go to the police. She had refused.

'They'll kill him anyway,' she had said with conviction. 'Either the army or our boys. I just have to wait.'

But in the end, it was she who died. One day two years ago. Her husband had killed her. Or so my father said. There was no proof. Everybody in the family said she killed herself.

My father had rushed to the village when one of her stepbrothers had come to him with the news. He saw her body.

'There was a lot of blood,' he said, his voice flat.

Two nights before she died, the army had come to the house and beaten her husband for helping the insurgents. And they had carried her away with them. They had kept her with them till the morning and she had walked back from their camp bloody and bruised. Nobody had talked to her.

'What could we say to her?' her in-laws had protested before my father.

For two days, she had kept washing herself in the pond behind the house. Between her baths, she would go to the tube-well, vomit, and wash out her mouth with soap.

'She kept scraping her tongue with her nails,' they said. 'Last night, she cut it off.'

'They said she bled to death, Maina,' my father looked at me. 'But if I know that girl, if that was the Romola we raised, she did not kill herself. I saw her husband. He had no remorse.'

His eyes were welling up with tears. My mother was crying too. But I could not. I did not feel bad for her at all. She had escaped. It did not matter that her husband had aided her escape.

I came back to Delhi soon afterwards. I decided I did not have to interview anybody else. I had Romola. I would write her story for the magazine.

When I told my husband about Romola, he hugged me. I cried into his shoulders.

'You should never have gone. It must have been so tough for you!' he whispered into my hair. For a while I forgot about everything else. I felt safe.

'That bastard should be shot dead! I really think staging an encounter for such people is justified,' he would say, every time he narrated Romola's story now. He did that at every party we went to for months thereafter. Everybody would then come up to me and say how sorry they were. I would smile back.

In one of the parties, we met the editor who had commissioned the story. I had not been responding to her emails. She was offended and asked me if I still intended to write the story. My husband said, 'We thought she should write Romola's story instead.'

She was mollified when she heard all of it and extended my deadline.

When we returned home, my husband said I owed him, and made me go down on him.

Despite all the toothpaste and mouthwash, I could still taste him on my tongue.

'Still, he's your husband,' I chided myself. 'Whose taste did Romola have on her tongue?'

As I walked out of the bathroom, wiping my mouth

with the back of my hand, I heard my phone beep. Then it beeped again. And then it went beep beep beep. With every beep, the volume kept rising. I had had it if it woke my husband up! He was sleeping peacefully now after all the drinks and all the exertion.

I finally traced the sound to my handbag hanging on the door. I desperately rummaged around inside it. I found my phone, and made a quick promise to myself to clear out the contents of the bag the next day and to organize it. I was going to dismiss the alert without even looking at it. But my eyes fell on the glowing blue text on the screen. 'Write Romola,' it said.

I had set this reminder many times earlier. But each time, I would say, 'Tomorrow,' and postpone it by another day, two days, a week. Today, I deleted it. If Romola wanted her story written, she would come sit beside me with her own notebook and pencil and read it out to me.

The Women Who Would Not Die

The plantain leaves were shivering in the wind. The women were seated around a dying fire. Their outstretched arms were warm, but their backs were starting to feel the chill. They knew they would soon have to get up. They knew they would soon have to go home. When they got home, they would each one of them push open their bamboo doors. The doors would creak on the hinges and they would pray the sound did not wake up their husbands and children. Then, in the dark, they would grope around till they found their beds of hay. As they lay down to wait for the morning, their bones would groan and creak too, but nobody would hear a sound.

Tonight was the night of the Kite but the Kite had not come. They had waited a long time, holding the fire responsible. The fire had kept their bodies warm, and warm bodies can sometimes feel hope. But the night had kept crawling over their skins threatening to seep in. Then feebly, from the distance, they had heard the *khong xinga* ringing. They had known then that the Kite would not come. They had been told she would be dead when that angry horn pipe rang. The happy pipe, the *rong xinga*, had turned to dust a long time back. Nobody had played its happy tune after the Kite's daughter died.

The Kite had a daughter once. She taught her how to laugh and talk, cook and clean, weave and sew, dance and sing, harvest and husk, hide and show. The perfect woman.

A man passing by under their tree one day found a strand of her hair on his shoulder. The Kite's daughter was combing her hair. He looked up and said he wanted to marry her. She played her *rong xinga* then and the Kite gave her her blessings.

After marriage, he took the Kite's daughter to his forest. It was across the border from the motherland.

The king of the motherland was a despot. He had a pack of wild dogs called the Rang Kukur.

The Kite's son-in-law was a rebel. The king's dogs chased him and his band of rebels and they took refuge in the forest. Other rebels from other lands had also taken refuge in the forest. It was in a no-man's land. Every man who was a rebel could live there. Every man who lived there, though, had to be an animal. The leader of the hill tribe, for instance, was a tiger-man. He said he would devour anybody who stood in the way of his people. The one leading the plain tribe was a lion who wore a ruby around his neck. He promised that after the war was over, he would pave the roads of his village with gold. The Kite's son-in-law led the people of the valley. He was a python.

When the Kite's daughter reached the forest, the women were all living there. They knew her husband was a python.

He had devoured his first wife in that form. The first wife's mother was a cat. When on their wedding night the husband had turned into the big snake, the cat's daughter had called out, 'Mother, my toes, they are a-tingling.'

The cat was in the motherland, dreaming of fish bones and warm milk. She sang back, 'Daughter, those are jewels a-dangling.'

The girl sang out again, 'Mother, my hand tingles.'

The cat crooned, 'Daughter, he gives you bangles.'

By the time the tingling reached her forehead, the cat's daughter had entered the belly of the beast.

On her first night, when the Kite's daughter sang out to her mother in the same way, the bird was alert, waiting for news from her daughter. When she heard her daughter's voice, she started flying. She reached in time to pull her out of the python's mouth. Her legs were covered in its digestive juices. In the morning, the python became a man and cried remorsefully. The Kite left.

The next night, the Kite was out hunting. When she heard her daughter sing out, she spread her long wings. She reached in time to pull her out of the python's mouth. She was covered up to her waist in its digestive juices. In the morning, the python became a man and again cried remorsefully. The Kite asked her daughter to leave. The girl stayed.

The night after that, there was a strong wind blowing. The Kite could barely hear what her daughter sang, but she took flight anyway. The wind kept pushing her back. She persisted. She reached in the morning but her daughter was dead. She played the *khong xinga* then, loud and shrill. And she turned to leave.

The sound of the *khong xinga* must have reached the motherland, for just then, the Rang Kukur howled. They were there, just across the border, ready to attack. The men prepared to run. The women were afraid. They stopped the Kite from leaving, told her about their sin. 'We didn't speak,' they said and spoke now.

The Kite told them to meet her by the plantain grove.

'I will come to you, any night, every night, wherever you are, whenever the plantain leaf shivers in the night wind,' she said and left.

The old bird had kept her promise. Even though the rebels were on the run, even though they travelled from one no-man's land to another, the Kite came to see the women wherever there was a plantain grove, every night the leaves shivered in the wind. And she taught them what she did not teach her daughter. She taught them how to grow feathers. She taught them how to fly. She taught them how to grow beaks and talons. She taught them how to rip and tear. And scratch and shriek and prey. She taught them how to evade the wild dogs that were on their scent still. She taught them how to master the wind.

That night, as the *khong xinga* rang again, they were in the hill of the dragons. They had been there for a fortnight now. The dragons were merciful. They said the pythons were their brothers and sheltered them. So the rebels from the plains now lived in the many caves of the hill of the dragons. Sometimes the women would wonder if they would ever descend to the valley again. Then they would tie their children tighter on their backs and walk carefully across the mountain stream.

That night, the Kite was supposed to teach them how to see. But she never came. Instead, they heard the *khong xinga* ring. Tomorrow, while bathing the children, cooking the rice, husking the paddy, sweeping the yard and milking the mithuns, the questions will sweep through their minds like so many spring storms: Who killed the Kite? Who blew the pipe? Who knew? Right now, though, they only watched the embers dying. Their eyes stung and they let the night in through the pores of their earth-coloured skin. Then they rose to leave.

Death has no meaning. It comes and somebody goes. Now that the Kite was gone, the women went about their next day's work as they were wont to. It was the nights that would be difficult. Whenever the plantain leaves shivered, they would think of her. They would look for meaning in her absence. They would find none.

As the day progressed, they killed the questions that were indeed sweeping through their minds one by one. Fetching water from the mountain spring, they watched one drown. Another was charred to death with the paddy husks. Yet another question was crushed to death with the mortar and pestle. By the time it was evening, they had resigned themselves and started accepting that from now on, their nights would be empty. Their feathers would have to be clipped, their wings folded and tucked away in the wooden boxes. Their collective sigh shook the hills, darkening now in the dusk.

Suddenly the hills seemed to come alive. They started ringing with the shrill notes of the *khong xinga*. For some time now, the sun had been trying quietly to penetrate the thin fabric of darkness that was lazily draping itself over the hills. Now, the Rang Kukur howled not very far away, and their cries tore the evening into a million multi-coloured shreds. It was war.

The rebels knew then that the dragons had been slain, for no man nor animal could mount the dragon hill while they stood guard in their submontane lairs. They waited for the Rang Kukur to arrive, for they also knew that there was no escape from the dragon hill. The only way down was the only way up and the Rang Kukur were on it. So they said they would fight unto death, but the women knew death wasn't pleasant.

'Maybe we can live,' they urged. But the men wanted to be heroes.

So the women tied their children to their backs and started walking down the hill. As they turned a bend, they saw the Rang Kukur approaching. They hid behind the trees. There was not a wind blowing. Not a leaf stirred. A small child whimpered in his sleep. The mother was afraid. But the Rang Kukur did not hear, for they were rejoicing loudly, blowing on the *khong xinga*. Their howls were cries of victory. Their victory was over the body of the Kite.

The women cringed behind the trees when they saw her, stripped to her skin, dragged by her feet, declawed, unfeathered, fettered. Blood oozed from her body, leaving a redder trail over the redness of the exposed earth that marked the hilly path. So she was not dead after all, they thought, just dying. And as they peered out at the procession, they saw her eyes searching for them. When they found them, they closed.

The women knew then that the Kite had given them the sight. That was to be her last lesson. So they spread out their wings and bared their talons. They took flight. The women rose above the trees, circling over the wild dogs. They shrieked with all their might and their shrieks dispersed whatever light remained in the hills.

Only eyes glowed now. Snake eyes, dog eyes, bird eyes. Snake eyes charged at dog eyes, dog eyes leapt in the air and snake eyes dimmed. And all the while, bird eyes circled overhead.

Soon, though, the children began to cry. Tied to their mothers' backs all this while, they were sleeping. Now they awakened. So the bird eyes glided away, breaking the circle, down the hills and into the valley below. The women were back in the motherland.

The next morning, they gathered twigs and leaves and built small nests for the children. And they settled down to wait for their husbands. They saw the Rang Kukur come down eventually and asked them, 'Where are our husbands?'

'We don't know,' they said.

'Did you kill them?' the women asked again.

'You don't kill snakes in the land of the dragon. We weren't even there.'

So the women flew up to the hills one day. There was nobody there. The shrubs and creepers and grasses had grown back up again, covering all traces of the war that was. They flew back down. And waited.

The king of the motherland came to meet them one day. He welcomed them back.

'You are home now,' he said.

'Where are our husbands?' they asked.

'Who?' said the king.

'Your wild dogs killed the Kite,' they said.

'Who?' he said again and went back to his palace.

Many people came to meet the women after that. Some offered them food and money. Some took their story to distant lands. They called the story 'The Kite and her daughters'. They marvelled at the children in their little nests of leaves and twigs.

'What craftsmanship!' they said.

Some called them resourceful, some lucky, others called them heroic.

'No,' they said emphatically. 'We are the women who did not die.'

[Inspired by the wives and children of the insurgents who went 'missing' after the 2003 Operation All Clear in Bhutan]

Body, Bones, and All

Winter: *Xeet*

I had a body once. It was scaly in winter when the cold sapped the moisture from my skin. One day, my father saw me scratching my legs from the ankle up to my buttocks. My frock was bunched up around my waist as the rice boiled behind me. The fire from the hearth made the itching worse. Later, when he sat down for his dinner, he said, 'Before you go to the river tomorrow, smear some mustard oil on your body.'

It worked. The itching stopped. Next morning, when I emerged from the waters, I felt like the water-fairy: the *jal kuwori* who could entice a prince. The river had washed away the scales and flakes. My skin was no longer like an old woman's. I hated old-woman skin. I was only thirteen. I had a long life to live. I was not my mother.

My mother had died giving birth to my little brother. But my little brother would not live without her. So he died too.

Her body was burnt in the backyard, at the furthest limit of our homestead. They piled the logs up in a small clearing behind the bamboo grove. The old kaji lime plant was cut down to make room. The fire burnt very hot. They wouldn't let me close to the fire. I wanted to see my mother burn, but they kept sending me back to the house. I went back to the pyre after the crowd broke. I saw some bones. Then my father came and carried me back to the house.

My brother was a baby, so he could not be burnt. They buried him beneath the bamboo grove. I did not see his bones.

Spring: *Boxonto*

In springtime, my body came to life, like Mother Earth waking from her slumber. Every Bihu we prayed to the pregnant Earth. We celebrated her fertility. We danced and feasted as though we had all just glibly flowed out of our mothers' wombs, announcing the end of winter. I had heard my mother screaming when my brother was born. I remember the pain.

But festivals always try to make you happy. They conspire to make you forget. And then this Bihu, I really felt fertile with new possibilities. I saw small hairs growing on my skin. I felt warm juices oozing out of my body, clinging to the hair, flowing down my legs. I stuck my hand between my legs to stem the tide. It did not help.

A pair of eyes, and then some more, started following me. To the river bank and back, dripping wet. To the paddy fields and mango groves, with friends who laughed. To school and walking back home, clutching the books to my bosom, now growing and tender to the touch.

At night, a soft whistle passing by my window made my skin tingle. I heard a plantain leaf shiver for no reason but that the wind touched it. Sometimes yellow moonlight pierced my body, while a dank distant voice whispered in my ear that pain could be pleasure too, if you let it be. Night after night, I lay awake in anticipation.

In the morning, though, I went out dancing with my friends. Because it was Bihu. We danced around the village, door to door, courtyard after courtyard. Our songs and our lithe bodies moving with the music reminded everyone about young love. They talked about love that lived in the heart, love that breathed in the open air, blossomed under the sun. But we knew the secrets of the night. Only we had seen the darkness in their souls. Our bodies, though, did not tell.

The seasons changed, and so did my body. I knew it was not my own, but I wasn't ready to give up on it yet. I shielded it, yet. Eyes, hands, breaths scorched it. Yet, I touched it. It needed reassurance. I was not ready to let it be crushed, yet.

Monsoon: *Borxa*

When the rains came, I was sixteen. Old enough to realize it was okay. If the body was crushed, it would become a creeper, a plant or a flower, and finally recover. Like Tejimola whose stepmother ground her, head after torso after feet after hands, with the foot pestle. My mother, long before she became a heap of ashes and some bones, told me the story. Every little boy and girl in our village was told the tale of Tejimola: the girl who refused to give up on living, coming back to life, again and again, shifting shape, and in the end, regaining her human form.

I would look for signs of my mother growing back up from the ground behind our house. But even the kaji lime tree refused to revive. They were both charred beyond resurrection. Or maybe my mother had just had enough of life. Unlike Tejimola, she stayed put.

My brother, though, grew roots among the bamboo. His baby bones that would have hardly been bones when he was buried, had hardened now and insinuated themselves into the gnarled base of the ancient bamboo grove. I liked that he did not give up, and he was only a baby. I would often go sit among the wet bamboo leaves and talk to him. He would understand and nod playfully, the lean bamboo swaying in the wind. My father would be taking his afternoon nap then.

'While you were sleeping, she grew up!' the villagers would tell him these days. But he wouldn't listen to them when they said I should get married. My body became the talk of the village and yet, my father refused to find a husband for me. At twenty, I was an old maid. 'Who will cook and clean if she leaves?' he reasoned. But they said, 'She's got two ripe oranges.'

My two ripe oranges had started straining against my blouse. When I lowered my head, my nose between them, I could smell a tangy smell rising up, tickling my nostrils. I would breathe it in and wait, sometimes in old-woman skin, sometimes washing off, desperately, like the water-fairy. I did not know what it was I waited for.

And then one day, my father said I should get married. I was twenty-two.

The lame fox got married on a rainy day when the sun was out, and we all reddened our lips with betel juice.

We sang this song when we were kids. Now, I was

marrying the lame fox, my friends joked, because it was a rainy day and the sun was shining, and I was marrying the gunman.

Everybody called him the gunman, but nobody had seen his guns. They knew, though, that he used to hide them under his bed for the rebels to pick up later. That was why he had been beaten up so badly in the army camp. Now he could not walk straight.

After the wedding was over, and the fun and laughter had died down, he limped across the village to his house. I walked slowly by his side.

Summer: *Grismo*

It isn't that marriage is such a bad thing; the body sometimes bloomed. Like the roses that braved the summer heat even though their colours faded in the sun. But pretty soon, I stopped seeing the point of it.

If being married meant I had to go from one house to another and be myself all over again, why did they say I would be starting a new life? I missed talking to my brother. My father had metamorphosed into my husband. Would I become my mother now? I didn't think so. My mother remained dead. I still wanted to live. And sleep one full night.

But the nights were when the bad dreams awakened in the gunman. There were no guns under his bed now, only the dreams. And they crawled out after dark and kept us awake at night. My body became his battlefield. The rebels dug deep furrows on my skin, the army dragged me by my hair. He shouted abuses at them. The abuses flowed through my veins like blood we had witnessed flowing down the streets during the army operations.

Every morning, my husband woke up and apologized. The lame fox in the rain when the sun was out. His tears healed my wounds, every morning. 'I have endured a lot, you must understand,' he told me, and I understood.

But the more I understood, more night turned into day, and battery into a habit.

Habituated, the body starts realizing: eyes, ears, nose, skin and bones, how fragile, how brittle they are! And yet, sometimes, how cleverly mending, how dramatically reshaping! They break and mend unlike earthen pots and pans flung on the walls. They can be cut open and stitched back up, like the tapestry in the prayer room. But they cannot be burnt and singed and yet leave behind the fragrance of incense. They cannot bleed and dry without also drawing a few tears, a few whimpers, which float around and follow you to the pond, into the kitchen, behind closed doors, in the front yard.

Not that anybody cares. Why, even the body doesn't care! It is so adapting, so accommodating. It finds ways to attenuate the importance of being beaten and bruised. It learns to absorb: blows, blame, branding. Yes, even that: even the words that slice through your soul, sharpest of all. It becomes impenetrable. It keeps the darkness at bay. It makes you feel like you are winning. Bad dreams wouldn't come to me. Like they wouldn't come to my mother who didn't want to dream herself into another life.

Autumn: *Xorot*

But I did not want to be like my mother. She died before she could live. I was twenty-five. I had life, still.

My body, though, started changing, transforming, as if preparing for the bone-chilling cold of the coming seasons. Cooking by the fire, fetching water from the river, washing and cleaning, preening and cajoling, it had always pretended to be mine. Now, though, ever so often, it started escaping. It would not be admonished, it would not be contained.

Sometimes it became fire and water; at other times, it reduced itself to dust and ash. And often, it just merged with the sky, or the green. At times, it quietly vanished and I remained disembodied, watching as my husband ran at me with a piece of firewood, or his bare hands. It did not hurt, there were no scars, because my body would abandon me, ever so kindly, just then.

Its kindness, of course, had nothing to do with me. It wasn't doing what it was for me. It was simply growing into that ancient art our ancestors had mastered: of transmogrification. They said it manifested itself in a few, that not everybody got the gift. I was glad I did. For now, words, hurtful words, bounced off my skin to become so many blue and black butterflies. Blows, strong blows, touched my skin and lo, underneath bloomed a thousand splendid roses, crimson and scarlet. I gagged on my husband's juices, and a river flowed through me. On the waters, there floated a song. I shackled my soul to that song. My mother sang it to me. I sing it to my son. It was a song about a river that flows free.

Pre-winter: *Hemonto*

Freedom, of course, comes at a cost. The cost of freedom, for me, was one dead baby. Another body for burial, another bamboo grove. No resurrection this time. It was a season to embrace death, not lust after life. The dead were wiser, the living not so much.

When the next child survived, I determined to teach him how to fly. Holding him close in the warmth of the kitchen, I showed him how the smoke always escaped the fire. It flew away. When his father flung him from me, I said, he should become like the smoke. He should fly away.

But babies, it seems, are not very smart. My son refused to learn. He fell with a thud, every time. And cried. I didn't like that. It wasn't a sound to inspire the living.

I also didn't like it that babies didn't think of consequences. Like my baby brother who grew back up as a bamboo plant and my father just cleared up the entire grove to build a new house when he remarried. So much for not going away, I thought. So much for wanting to stay home. My mother's bones are floating in some river far away from home. Once upon a time, long long ago, my father collected them and went on a pilgrimage and drowned them where three rivers met. She never came back. She must be happy where she is.

The thought of her happiness made me sad. I wanted my babies to be happy. And me too. So I dug up my dead baby one night and burnt him to his bones. My living son whimpered in my arms. The flames were too hot. So I took him down to the cool waters of the river. The river taunted me. It promised me freedom, if only I took with me my song.

I did.

So now, I have a body no more.

Again, Winter: ***Akou Xeet***

A few villages down, an old woman sits beside the fire. Having grown into her old-woman skin, she has tales to tell. Tonight, her story is about the water-fairy and her little prince. How body, bones and all, they walked into the river and flowed into the sea.

Colour Me Live

Black for the sky.

My dear sir, this is my sky. I can colour it whatever, however I want to now. It is my decision to make. Entirely personal. Your sky was a different colour. Under pressure from the rising sun, or in collaboration with the one setting, it took on all the different colours it ever could. But when you were with me, your sky always turned true blue, mirroring the turbulence of the river there, flowing by, down below. I asked you for the black. Repeatedly. Why couldn't you just give me that?

But I'm curious, sir. You were a poet, were you not? Why didn't you ever try to change the language of colours? Since our college days you kept me imprisoned in your words. You wrote poems on trees, rivers, flowers, the sun, the hills, and read them out to me. Your words started building their home in me. And one day, we got married and moved to this house of glass overlooking the river.

During our college days, I thought it was nice that your sky was psychedelic. Drunk on alcohol or high on marijuana, you would sing at the top of your voice, 'Lucy in the sky with diamonds'. I don't like diamond skies but since I loved you, I revelled in your sky. Only it wasn't yours, was it? You coloured your sky the way you made somebody else's words your own, adapting, adopting, ingratiating. But the skies, like the words, finally reveal themselves because everybody's own language (woven of words, colours, whatever) has its own peculiar, particular grammar. They do not, however, give themselves up so easily.

Words, especially, are liars, you know; they never own up. They never admit how insidious, invidious they can be.

Like the soft *ximolu* cotton, they waft off with every little breath, every small gust of wind. Like leaves fallen upon the river's waters, they flow hither and thither, wherever the river's current takes them. And yet, they are neither soft nor pliant. They leave behind the ghastliest of wounds in the deepest recesses of our souls.

We hold on to these wounds for as long as we live. We get beaten, we get burnt, we cry and we cringe, but we never quite fathom the intimate nature of the relationship between the words and the crafter who wields them against us. Bewildered, we watch as the words that are hurled at us hurriedly dissipate around us. Couldn't they, at least, leave behind a warning for us to not hold on to their meanings forever?

Even the river below is not forever. It is no solace; it just keeps flowing away. But maybe that is not so bad because sometimes, it takes with its flow the remnants of our many tinted deeds.

If life is the name of a river, muddy are the waters.

You claimed this very robust, very masculine river for your own, sir. Poetry, you said, is your mistress, and proclaimed to our guests on alcohol-charged evenings how you share her with the river, your friend and confidant. But when it rains on the hills above and the earth peels off of them, I sometimes wonder if the river is not really a woman. She turns red, brown, befuddled, muddled in the downpour, and yet, when it stops raining, she goes back to reflecting the feigned serenity of the blue skies above. Underneath, though, she remains seething, her heart heaving, her wounds unhealed. Why would she want to hide her wounds?

I wanted to hide my wounds from my son.

'He's only a baby,' you would say.

But, sir, babies know. They cry and fret; do not feed.

'Let's not do this in front of him,' I would say, 'take me to the other room.'

You would fling him from my arms and onto the bed. If only he could take flight then, I would wish, every time, in my mind. If only I could teach him how to fly away like the smoke I see rising from the hills beyond our river.

You would turn to me next, and my body would become your battlefield, your encounter ground to conquer, plunder, colour me red.

How I hate red! Some nights, your khaki policeman's uniform would be reeking of red when you came home. I would wash it immediately. I hated to see it in the morning, trying to appropriate my colour brown. Brown was for my river, my son, and me. Red I could sacrifice at the altar of your masculinity.

How often you brandished before me your two weapons of war: both big, both male, both loaded! And how knowledgeable, how intellectual you felt calling them that.

'This is a man's war. We will not be emasculated by a bunch of boys playing at being soldiers,' you would laugh as you reenacted how you dragged a pregnant woman by her hair and your men stomped on her belly till she revealed her husband's hideout. 'Everything is fair in love and war.'

More and more, your poetry had started courting platitudes. I cringed at your words and I clutched at my belly but I felt no pain, for my pain had sunk to the bottom of a swamp last night, weighted down by the exact number of bricks and stones required.

How powerful it made you feel, sir, the climax of your tale told between my thighs. You were indestructible. Death would do your bidding, ha ha!

'Bid death come for us,' I thought.

If we died, we could be free: we could both, mother and son, banish ourselves to the farthest reaches of the horizon, hidden away behind the grey clouds that meanwhile tickled the broad sky red or orange or pink. The grey would be for us—to keep us safe. The rest would be there only for the world to see.

The world, after all, needs its rose-tinted glasses. It needs to see a man capable: strong, sensitive, decisive. It needs to see a woman happy, in marriage, in motherhood. It needs to see a child smile. And to put them all in a lavish, cosy house made of glass on the edge of the river. No matter if a few window panes needed changing every few weeks. No matter if the TV needed to be replaced every now and then, or the telephone, or even the bookcases. Too much money, the world would say and pass on.

I, sir, could not learn such detachment, such deception. I wanted to die.

Then one night, the grey clouds burst. You dragged me down to the edge of the river to show me how angry it was. How angry it would be if I did not submit. Nobody heard your war cries or my screams because the river herself was tumbling down the hills that were unable to contain it any longer. I wanted to get back to my son. At that moment, I did not want to die because if I did, what kind of life would he have with you?

I did not even have to push too hard and suddenly, you became a fallen leaf, drowning, surfacing, flowing hither and thither with the current.

Can you believe it, sir? I smiled through the rain as I climbed up the river bank, back to the house. Our son was sleeping quietly. I lay down beside him.

When tragedy strikes young women leaving them grieving widows, an infant in their arms, the world empathizes.

'He should never have gone near the river when the skies were breaking open. That river is a wild one.'

They told me I should cry: 'But you must! It is cathartic.'

True, I thought, and I cried. For many days thereafter.

But now that it is all out of my system, sir, I think I will kohl-line my eyes. Now that I will not need to cry anymore, it will not run. Now, I shall have the black with me forever. To colour my eyes, my sky, or whatever.

Now I shall have my black, to colour me live.

Beloved of Flowers

As Dino turned to close the rickety iron gate behind him, he felt a drop of something cold fall on the back of his hand. He shuddered. He looked up and realized it was a dewdrop. He felt a strong urge to reach out and touch the tiny drops that he saw dripping from the translucent petals of the purple flowers overhead. The flowers seemed alive, articulate, about to break into a tale of tormented love, or hate, or perhaps of how love and hate are so often so intertwined in our lives.

Dino felt a shooting pain in his heart at that bittersweet thought. He made a mental note to use it in the next story he wrote. These last few days, it was as if he had been living from one story to the next. He had wanted to continue writing without a break and not be distracted but then he had been summoned to the big house. He had walked over the hill and down again, grudgingly, clinging to the broad strap of the cloth bag hanging from his shoulder. His pen and white ream of paper were tucked away in the bag.

But here was a new story the flowers were telling him now, if only he could hear it and record it. They were blooming breathlessly on the bare body of the nearly leafless climber that had twisted itself around the iron archway stretching from one concrete pillar to the other on either side of the gate. Dino could not move. He stood there, looking up.

'Let it be, *kon goxai*! The gate seems to have grown a mind of its own,' Kuxumpriya Baruani *baideu*'s command reached him from the veranda of the house at the end of the driveway.

Dino's trance was broken. With one mighty effort, he managed to align the two halves of the gate and fix the L-shaped latch in the middle. He could not just leave it open: that would be most unseemly.

He folded his hands in greeting as he walked down the short driveway to approach the matriarch of the famous Barua clan of Guwahati. In the early days, after the British left, the family owned nearly half of the land in Guwahati, and then some outside the lazily growing city. Till this day, it lived off the land—cultivating some, selling some. And there was more left to spare.

'Who's going to feed off all that land once the old lady's dead?' Tarinikanta often complained. He was Dino's neighbour and now, his best friend in the city. 'Of course, if she had a daughter, I would marry her and look after all the property myself,' he would joke. 'I would take care of that imbecile son of hers too.'

Dino would smile, but never allow the joke to stretch on. And he would wonder, about the daughter…

As he stood in front of the woman now, it suddenly struck him that she must be hardly five feet tall. And yet, Dino always felt small in front of her. He felt as though everybody looked small and insignificant in front of her. Everybody except, of course, his elder brother, Sri Sri Dayananda Debo Goswami, the spiritual head of the Barbari *xattra*. Kuxumpriya Baruani *baideu* was his disciple.

His elder brother, whom he called Dangor da, had founded the religious institution at Barbari on his own, having cut himself off from their original *xattra* in Gohepara. By the time Dino was old enough to go to school, Dangor da had already left the parent *xattra,* and ever since, Dino had grown up hearing about his exploits. In local lore, just as in Dino's mind, his elder brother had become something of a legend. Tall tales were told of the vagabond *goxai*—the god among men—who moved from district to district, giving refuge to whole communities of converts and setting up branches of his own *xattra*. Their father, the old or *bura goxai*, had set up just one house of god in his lifetime, but Dangor da already had three. And even though he did not have a *xattra* in Guwahati, he had as his disciples some of the richest, most aristocratic families in the city, who often arrived at his remote *xattras* looking for spiritual guidance in their dust-covered motor cars.

Many years ago, on one rare occasion, when Dino had gone to Dangor da's Barbari *xattra*, Kuxumpriya *baideu* had come looking for the *goxai*. Morning prayers had just been concluded and the disciples had left for their homes. Dino and a few other boys were playing a game, running in and out of the prayer hall. Suddenly, there was a commotion outside the *xattra* and one of Dangor da's disciples, Ramani *bhakat,* had rushed in to announce the arrival of the lady with the delicately poetic name: Kuxumpriya, Dino recalled from a poem they had studied in school that year, meant 'beloved of flowers'.

He had run out to the road with the other village children just in time to see the woman who bore the name alighting from her once-white-now-grey-with-dust Premier Padmini. Dressed in a white *mekhala-sador* radiant with metallic gold motifs, she had looked like a queen to him, quite formidable, nothing delicate or flower-like about her. Then, when this regal personage had entered the *namghor* and bowed before his own brother, touching his feet, seeking his blessing, Dino had felt as if his heart would burst with pride.

It had taken a while for the awe to settle down and give way to curiosity. When it did, Dino had studied her entourage. It comprised of two ladies in waiting and a young girl, about Puni bai's age. For a brief moment, his heart ached for his elder sister who had been the one person in the family to make him feel loved. Without her sunny presence, he felt abandoned. The girl seated on the *namghor* floor now was nothing like his sister; she looked pale and sickly, and distinctly uncomfortable.

One of the two ladies sat directly behind *baideu*, fanning her with an intricately woven bamboo fan. The other fussed over the folds of the girl's *mekhala-sador*, ironing the pale pink silk between her fingers. When she was not doing that, she was wiping the sweat beads off the girl's forehead with a matching pink handkerchief. Dino could make out from the tormented look on the girl's face that she did not enjoy any of this. She kept pushing away the attending lady's hands and tugging at her *sador*, pulling it closer around her body. If she was married, she would have covered herself from head to toe, wrapping the loose end of the long *sador* over her head like Kuxumpriya *baideu* did. And if she did, Dino felt, she would become a heap of silver flowers floating, gleaming on a stretch of pink silk. The perfect offering for the *goxai*.

The girl kept stealing looks at the children who were leaning in from every available window in the *namghor*, pushing and shoving against each other in their eagerness to witness the ceremony being performed inside. Like them, Dino too could not make head or tail of what was happening between *bhakatani*, *goxai* and god in the *monikut*, the sanctum sanctorum of the prayer hall. Being the youngest of four sons, he was not expected to take over his father's *xattra*. And so, he remained as yet uninitiated. Nobody really bothered with him when it came to imparting the familial knowledge, traditions and rituals of the *xattra* institution. Besides, he was the first among all of the *bura goxai*'s sons to complete primary schooling and go to middle school. His teacher, Khonin mastor, said he had high hopes for Dino and had even made a strong supplication to his father to allow the youngest heir to go for higher education whereby he could spread the glory of the *xattra* far and wide through the written word. Strangely enough, the *bura goxai* had agreed. Dino would be leaving for Patkusi soon to enroll in the high school there. Dangor da had arranged for his stay with one of his disciples at Patkusi.

Dino had no idea about what to expect once he left Gohepara. But he was excited. Dangor da had summoned him only yesterday to tell him that if he could complete high school, he would make arrangements for Dino to go to Guwahati! As he sat facing his elder brother in front of the *monikut*, Dino had suddenly felt something akin to filial affection towards him: as though his brother was a benign patriarch, and he, a beloved son. All his life, he had only known awe and amazement towards this man. Now that he felt an almost earthly sentiment creeping into his heart, it gave him, at the same time, a nagging sense of guilt. Dangor da was above such human affections; he was, like their father, a god among men: to be adored, but with admiration; to be worshipped and held in awe.

The kind of awe he now saw Kuxumpriya Baruani *baideu* holding him in, clinging to his every word, following every instruction in performing the ongoing ritual, bowing to his commands. The girl who came with her, however, seemed more interested in what was going on outside.

'*Aijoni*, little mother, what is your name?'

Dangor da had to repeat his question before the woman attending to the girl shook her by her feet. 'Tell *goxai deu* your name!' she said in a whisper loud enough for everybody to hear.

'Tejassini Barua,' the girl blurted out loudly, caught off guard.

Dangor da turned his back to her then and continued chanting the benedictions, uttering her name every now and then.

Dino liked the name, although he did not know what it meant. He wanted to know more about her and wondered if she was Kuxumpriya *baideu*'s daughter. Why was she so sad? Maybe he could talk to her. Would she talk to him? People from the city did not normally waste their time on village bumpkins like him.

But then he remembered he was not a village bumpkin, was he? He was the son of the *xatrradhikar* Sri Sri

Gopalsandra Debo Goswami, and the younger brother of Sri Sri Dayananda Debo Goswami. How could *he* be considered a bumpkin? He was not like these common village boys at all. It was beneath him, the little god—*kon goxai*—to be thus aligning himself with these lesser mortals. What was he doing peeping in through the window anyway? If he wished, he could go sit by his brother and offer the same benedictions. Why was he demeaning himself this way?

As the thought started gripping his mind and growing, Dino found himself grinding his teeth silently. He turned away from the window, but stopped short. For two brief seconds, his eyes clashed and held with the girl's. They were empty. Puni bai's eyes always reminded him of the *doyar xagor*—oceans of kindness—that the hymn talked about. And he loved how much love they held for him, always. But without understanding why, this girl's eyes surprised him with their barrenness.

As he walked out of the *xattra* towards the street outside, a strange sadness started descending upon Dino. He started feeling very heavy. It was as if, suddenly, his shoulders could not carry the weight of his being; he felt bogged down by dark clouds of immense sorrow. Of late, he had felt that happening to him more and more often. When it did, all he wanted to do was crawl into a corner and cry.

Just then, though, surrounded by so many people, he could not. So he sat under the bokul tree a little distance away from the *xattra* entrance. After a short while, the rituals must have ended for the crowd started slowly moving out of the *namghor* courtyard. From his vantage point, Dino saw Dangor da and Kuxumpriya *baideu* come out of the *namghor* and walk towards the pond in the backyard. They were deep in conversation.

Dino's heart suddenly started beating faster. He saw a few boys from the village approach the car and begin to draw faces and ugly sceneries on its dusty bonnet with their fingers. His heart filled with trepidation as he watched, from his safe distance, the boys' grand act of subversion. What would happen when the city lady finished conferring with Dangor da? He sat there dreading that any minute now the driver of the car would come charging at them with a stick.

That did not happen, however, and when Kuxumpriya Baruani *baideu* and her entourage had finally driven off, their hair now white with dust, Dangor da had explained to the naughty village boys that being aristocratic also meant being large of heart; but the next time they defaced any of his disciples' cars, they would have to deal with him. Dino had been glad he had not joined the boys earlier.

Many years later, when he moved to Guwahati to enroll in Cotton College, he realized the truth of Dangor da's words about aristocracy and large-heartedness. For the first few months, he had lived in a room with bamboo walls and a thatched roof that let the rains in and dampened his bed, his clothes, and worst of all, his books. He had spent many nights awake, worrying that the thin plastic covering he had retrieved from the roadside behind his college would fail to protect his books from the heavy rains. He could dry out his clothes the next morning over the kerosene stove his landlady had so graciously provided. He did not mind that they would stink of kerosene for days afterwards: he never noticed how his classmates sniggered when he walked by. But he could not allow the destruction of his books, bought with the money he earned from giving tuitions to the sons and daughters—some his own age—of the city's rich and famous.

Many of those whose houses he visited every evening to give tuitions—and also to save on his dinner expense—were disciples of his elder brother. They were extremely gracious to him and treated him with utmost respect, laying out clean *gamosas* for him to wipe his hands with and serving him food only in bell metal utensils. But he never allowed them to know about his predicament. Kuxumpriya *baideu,* though, heard about it one day from a disciple of Dangor da's who was delivering the *goxai*'s benedictions to her in the city. She had immediately sent her chauffeur to seek him out and moved him to one of her own properties behind the hill.

Barua Asthan was a sizeable plot of land, next to the World War II Cemetery below the Nabagraha Hill. It was fenced and gated, with a small house in the middle. The house had a tin roof and walls made of mud plastered over river rushes like most other houses in the city, except of course, of the very rich who had started moving into brick-and-mortar houses in recent years. His benefactress had been one of the first to do so.

As he drove him and his meagre possessions to the house, the chauffeur informed Dino that he had heard that *baideu* used to live in the same house till her husband was alive. He had died six years ago, leaving her with an infant son, born late in life.

'He's retarded, you know,' the driver whispered, loudly, as is proper when revealing a secret.

'And her daughter?' Dino asked, suddenly remembering those empty eyes, from what? Was it six or seven years ago now?

'She has no daughter,' the driver answered, his tone patient. Obviously, this village boy knew nothing about the family.

Dino felt embarrassed he had even asked. He had assumed that the girl who had accompanied Kuxumpriya Baruani *baideu* to Barbari was her daughter. He had been so sure. He ground his teeth now, silently, angry at having made a fool of himself. He decided to ride the rest of the distance in silence. The chauffeur, however, talked ceaselessly, pointing out the various landmarks of the city. Dino kept making appropriate noises of acknowledgement and gratitude at timely intervals, letting the chauffeur presume he was new in town.

When they reached Barua Asthan, Dino found that the house had been divided into three units. Dino had been given the room on the cemetery side. The room in the middle was occupied by a high school teacher, Tarinikanta Deka. They were to share everything—the makeshift kitchen constructed in the back veranda as well as the bathroom; and beyond that, they also shared the same love of literature and writing. They bonded within a very short time over long evenings spent discussing books and making dire predictions about the future of Axamiyā literature. The third unit, on the far end, comprised of two rooms and the main kitchen and bathroom. It had apparently been vacated some time back and new tenants were expected soon. But for as long as Dino lived there, the new tenants never came, and that portion of the house remained locked up.

Barua Asthan was further away from Dino's college than his earlier place, but Dino did not mind the long walk. It gave him a chance to meet and greet a lot of people along the way, and to observe life in the city closely. He had started writing stories for a few local tabloids and weekly newspapers: he found that it was a good way to earn some extra money. Of course, he wrote under a pseudonym for he did not want anybody in his family, or any of the *xattra* disciples for that matter, knowing how the youngest *goxai* wrote candidly about the material life in the city or about the youthful desires that its pale lights ignited in the restless hearts of lonely souls. He also wrote under an assumed name because he was not entirely sure he should indeed be writing on such subjects: he *was*, after all, the *goxai*'s son, a little god himself, who should instead be contemplating upon spirituality and the deeper meanings of life.

But ever since coming to the city, Dino had found himself getting more and more intrigued by the sheer carnality that hid itself in the unlit crevices of the city. The city was growing on him, day after day, month after month. He wanted to hate it, and maybe he did hate it too, but it would not leave him be. Like a living organism, it seeped into his soul, assaulted his senses, captivated his sensibility, till he did not know what it was he hated more: the city that would not let him be, or himself, who could not remain content with who he was born to be.

'*Goxai*, you worry too much,' Tarinikanta would chide him. He was the only one who knew Dino's secret and he was also the reader of his first drafts.

'You are going to be a great writer one day, and that is all that should matter to you. That is your destiny. Not the *xattra* for you, my friend—that is your Dangor da's destiny—but the annals of our living literary tradition.'

'It is sleaze, Tarini, sleaze. That is what I write. It is not literature,' in his dark moments, Dino would lament.

'Where I come from, we talk of love and surrender, not lust and gruesome death. We talk of crossing over from this world to the next, not getting caught in the web of fancy woven by those that know not the Most High!'

'My friend, as your critic, counsellor and champion, let me tell you this: I see you rising above it all, like the lotus that blooms in the mud. You shall overcome.'

Dino was not so sure.

And then, just last month, a publishing house of some repute had approached him through one of the tabloids he wrote for and requested a manuscript of his unpublished stories. Dino had started writing then, furiously, determined to live up to his friend's predictions. He had been given a chance and he had to be the lotus that bloomed in the mud. Being summoned to the big house had come as an irritant, but now that the flowers had spoken to him, maybe there was a story there too. The flowers had reminded him of a tale he had heard one day as a little boy, of a young girl who had grown into a plant, blossomed into a flower, become a lotus...

At their *xattra*, it had always been tales from the scriptures that one heard. But that day, he had heard Ramen kaka's mother telling her grandchildren the tale of an unfortunate girl killed by her stepmother.

Puni bai had been unwell and had sent him to Ramen kaka's house to fetch a homeopathic medicine he had brought for her from Guwahati. She had cautioned him to be very careful not to let anybody at the *xattra* or in the village know about it. If they found out the daughter of Xattradhikar Sri Sri Gopalsandra Debo Goswami was ingesting medicine prepared by doctors from the city, she would be excommunicated; or worse still, made to go through all those excruciating cleansing ceremonies again.

Dino had been cautious for his sister's sake, making his way to Ramen kaka's house in the pitch darkness without a lamp. When he reached kaka's courtyard, he found the entire family huddled around a fire. When kaka saw him at the *nangala mukh*, he quickly stood up: 'Come in, come in, *kon goxai*. Come and have a seat inside.'

Dino enjoyed being the son of the spiritual leader of the community: it made him feel important, especially since even the elders called him a god. He always got special treatment in people's houses, and that included being made to sit separately from other children.

But today he would have much preferred to sit around the fire with Ramen kaka's children and listened to Golapi *abu's* stories. As he waited for kaka to wrap the medicine in a piece of old newspaper, he heard the old woman's voice drift in through the thinning mud walls that were letting the light from the fire filter into the house, here and there, piercing through its bamboo skeleton. She had just started a new story, something about a girl named Tejimola.

Suddenly, Ramen kaka rudely interrupted everybody. He said in a raised voice from the threshold, 'Here, *kon goxai,* here is the new book I got for you from Guwahati.'

Dino rose from the wobbly wooden bed he was seated on and held his right hand out. As his fingers closed around the newspaper wrapping, he ground his teeth silently. He mumbled something under his breath and started towards the *nangala mukh*.

As he passed the children huddled around the fire, though, his feet slowed down. He did not realize when they had stopped moving altogether, but there he was, listening to the saddest story he was to ever hear in his lifetime. The young girl, beautiful, so full of life, going to her friend's wedding and returning with her stepmother's silk clothes in tatters. The stepmother's feigned anger—for it was she who had hidden the mice in the folds of her own clothes that she had lent Tejimola—made Dino truly angry. He moved closer to the fire and without knowing it, sat down.

'*Eh*, *goxai*'s son! *Hoh*, don't sit on the ground; take this pira,' Golapi *abu* paused in her narrative long enough to scoop out the low wooden stool from under her buttocks and hand it to Dino. Nobody else said anything. Nobody else existed for them right now but the tragic little girl, tearful and terrified.

Dino felt tears stinging his eyes when the stepmother ground Tejimola to death with a mortar and pestle and threw her remains in the backyard. Hope sprung up in his breast beating back the imminent tears when she grew into a fruit-bearing plant only to be cut down again. And then again, when she grew into a flowering creeper, and was cut down and thrown into the river. Dino thought his heart would burst with anger and fear and hope and joy and love and tenderness and so many other emotions he knew not what to name as the old woman took her listeners on the rollercoaster ride of the wretched little girl's rising and falling fortunes until in the end, her lust for life triumphs. Overcoming multiple deaths, she floats finally on the river as a lovely lotus flower. Her father returning home by boat reaches out to pluck the flower and it sings out to him: '*Don't you reach out, don't you pluck me...*'

When the flower finally convinces the father: 'It is me, Teji', she returns to her old form. Dino remembered imagining a young girl rising up from the water, her tresses wet like Puni bai's after her morning bath, her thick white cotton *mekhala-sador* clinging to her as she trudged water on her way to the river bank. He also remembered feeling a sweet sadness that Tejimola's adventures were now over. He found no consolation in the stepmother's nose being cut off by the father, or her being banished to another land. All he could think about as he made his way back to the *xattra* that night, the contraband tied to his waist under the knot of his dhuti, was Tejimola's sad eyes as she emerged from the waters. He realized he could not discern what this sadness was all about: was it because even in death, she found no respite? Or was it, instead, because her post-human life adventures were now over? All he did know was that Tejimola's story affected him like no other.

And now, standing in front of his benefactress, looking into her eyes as each greeted the other with folded hands, his mind travelled back again to another pair of eyes, empty, lifeless. Who was she? Where *was* she? With uncharacteristic recklessness, Dino determined to find out.

'Where have you been hiding, *kon goxai*?'

The matriarch's tone was sharp, expressing a deep disappointment. She had sent her chauffeur to summon him last week, but Dino had been unable to tear himself away from his writing.

'Tell her I'll be there,' he had said and continued writing.

He had not been attending college or going for his tuitions as well. Tarini had tried to coax him to join him for a meal a couple of times, but given up when he realized Dino wanted to be alone with his writing.

'My friend, I shall not stand as the obstruction in your path to greatness,' he had finally announced, in his usual theatrical manner, and withdrawn.

This morning, however, the chauffeur had banged on his door again and offered to drag him bodily to the big house, if required.

'Reach there by noon, or I will be back,' he had threatened as he left.

Dino had shuffled around then, looking for his sandals and making his way to the bathroom in the backyard. He could not remember when he had last bathed. He did not want to bathe now; he felt his stories might wash away with the bath water. But he also knew that if he did not take a bath, he would fall into sin because Kuxumpriya *baideu* usually called him to the house these days if she needed him to read from the scriptures.

Dino did not know how much she knew about his ignorance of the *xattra* rituals, but he thought it best not to draw undue attention to it. He had a strong voice, no doubt inherited from his father, and he could sing well from the scriptures and that seemed to suffice for his benefactress. Since she did not have a dedicated prayer room with a *monikut,* she would lay out a *thapona* instead and observe all the rituals around the makeshift altar in a practiced manner: she had been Dangor da's disciple for a long time now. But since Dangor da could not come into the city very often, she had taken to calling upon his younger brother instead.

Kuxumpriya Baruani had taken refuge in the elder *goxai*, no doubt, but that did not mean that she could not berate his younger brother. She showed him all the reverence due to a member of the *goxai*'s family, but was too used to the deference she herself received from everybody around her to allow a lesser god to disobey her diktat.

'Please accept my apologies, *baideu*. I wasn't hiding; I was writing. I have a manuscript due soon...' Dino's voice trailed away before the matriarch's direct gaze.

Suddenly, her eyes softened, and her whole body relaxed. She was a benign matriarch again, his benefactress.

'Good to know you are writing, *kon goxai*. You must tell me more about it.'

But the finality in her tone did not indicate any real desire to know anything more about his writing ever, at all. Dino was relieved. He had blurted out his secret, without even realizing it.

He followed her into the house and she indicated a chair which had a new *gamosa* spread out on it.

'Sit,' she said, softly.

Dino complied.

She lifted a curtain and walked out of the room through a door next to where Dino sat. For a long time, he could only hear distant voices and the faint clinking noises of utensils from behind the curtain, somewhere deep within the house.

This was the first time Dino had been kept waiting. On the two or three earlier occasions that *baideu* had summoned him to her house, she had had the *thapona* ready on the floor in the far corner of the living room, the *gamosa* laid out over the rug that was to be his seat, and the holy book open at the page she wanted him to recite from. He would offer his prayers, recite from the book and when that was done, eat the food served to him there, on the floor. *Baideu*'s maid would have packed some of the offerings for him in his bag by the time he was ready to leave. When he stood up to leave, both *baideu* and her maid would kneel on the floor and touch his feet. He would say a blessing, like he had seen his father and Dangor da do, and take a deep breath when he had finally turned his back on the house.

Today *baideu* did not need him to read from the book, and Dino suddenly felt a sense of panic wondering what it was that she did require of him. He sat there, feeling his heart palpitate, when there was a slight movement behind the curtain screening the door on the far wall from where Dino sat. Dino cleared his throat, thinking it might be the lady herself. But a little hand shot out from behind the curtain and drew it aside.

For the first time, Dino saw Kuxumpriya Baruani *baideu*'s son. He was small for his age—and Dino had been told he was about six or seven. At first glance, he looked normal enough and Dino could not understand why everybody said there was something wrong with him. All Dino found different about him was that he wore a thick pair of glasses. They made his eyes look big and bulging.

When he emerged from behind the curtain, the little boy was smiling. The smile remained fixed on his face as Dino and he stared at each other from their respective positions, and neither of them moved for a long time. It was an innocent smile, but it disconcerted Dino. Finally, he called out, 'Come here, babu. What is your name?'

The little boy moved forward slowly, cautiously, and when he was close enough, swiftly clambered up to Dino's lap and sat there with his head on Dino's chest, sticking his thumb in his mouth. Dino was taken aback. He did not know what to do.

'Are you sleepy?' he ventured. 'Shall I call your mother?'

The boy only shifted his head a little to study Dino's face. As he did so, his glasses were lifted from his eyes. Dino's breath suddenly left him as he found himself looking into a pair of eyes he had found clashing with his so many years ago at Barbari *xattra*.

'Is he bothering you, *kon goxai*?' Kuxumpriya *baideu* walked in just then. She was followed by her maid who was carrying a tray laden with tea and snacks which she laid on the table next to Dino.

'Please help yourself, *goxai deu,*' the maid said, and knelt before him, touching his feet.

Dino muttered a prayer under his breath, touched his hand to her head and said, '*Hoise, hoise,* you can get up now.'

As the maid withdrew behind the curtain, Kuxumpriya Baruani lifted the little boy off of Dino's lap. He went without protest. Dino's head was reeling, and he was having difficulty breathing. From somewhere far away, *baideu*'s voice was floating in towards him.

'His name is Gungun, *goxai.* Everybody said I should not have a baby so late in life, that I should be ashamed of myself, but I couldn't kill an unborn child. Now look, he is paying the price for it...'

Her voice trailed away as Dino slowly started regaining his composure. He looked at woman and child seated across the room from him. Gungun was curled up, quietly, in the ageing woman's lap the same way he had been in Dino's.

This woman, seated in front of him now, was not the same formidable person who had met him at the front veranda not so very long ago. She looked frail. That gave Dino courage.

'And your daughter?' he asked.

Baideu looked up, startled. But she quickly regained her poise.

'So you remember her? I thought you might not. That would have been easier.'

Dino realized it was not proper to feel a sense of jubilation at such a moment, but he felt something akin to self-pride creeping into his heart as he waited for the old lady to elaborate.

In the same tired voice, she continued, 'She was ashamed of me, *kon goxai*. Her own mother! When she heard I was having a baby, she ran away from home. She left a note, you know, and she left. I haven't seen her since. No one remembers her. There was this engineer, a Gujarati boy, who had been following her around in college. She must have left with him. We do not talk about her anymore. It is best not to. She is dead to us...'

A tear escaped from behind her glasses. Dino felt very uncomfortable. He did not know if he should say something, but a deep sense of guilt or remorse or some other emotion he could not recognize just yet was rising in his throat and he could not speak.

'I had the baby prematurely, immediately after she left. My husband left us too, soon after. He was a good man, did a lot for the community. Everybody loved him. He died in his sleep one day, peacefully. He did not suffer,' *baideu*'s voice trailed away.

Involuntarily, Dino took a deep breath. It made a deafening sound.

Baideu looked up from where she sat.

'Only Gungun and I were left behind, tied to each other by birth and death.'

Dino was afraid she might start crying again. That would be most embarrassing. Thankfully though, she just sat there, in front of him, head bowed again, in silence. The little boy sucked his thumb, his head tucked safely in *baideu*'s bosom.

After a long time, the matriarch raised her head and looked directly at Dino.

'You will not discuss any of this with my servants though, will you? They are new and they do not know. I'm telling you all this because you are family. You deserve to know. Your Dangor da has been the greatest source of strength and succour for me through all this. You will keep my trust?'

Dino hastened to assure her he would never talk about any of this.

'You can trust me, *baideu*,' he said.

'Good then, have your tea. It's gone cold. Shall I have it heated for you again?' But she did not wait for him to respond and held the cup up for him.

Dino took the cup from her and sipped the cold tea.

'Now to business,' she announced, suddenly back to her old self. 'You must be wondering why I've called you here today?'

'I was...' Dino started, but she cut him short.

'I want you to tutor Gungun. Can you do that?'

It was not so much a question as a command, and Dino knew he would have to do her bidding whether he wanted to or not.

'I'll pay you of course...'

'No, no,' Dino started to protest, but she continued as though she had not heard him.

'You will come in every Saturday and Sunday for an hour in the morning, and teach him the alphabet and numbers to start with. I need to make sure that after I'm gone, he can at least sign his name and do some basic calculations. I am not here forever, you know. Nobody is. So he is in your charge from now on.'

Dino realized he had been given his instructions and dismissed. He rose to leave, his heart heavy, fearful. He did not want to come to this house again, ever again, but he also knew he was being given no choice.

As he descended the few steps from the veranda into the driveway, making his way toward the gate, he found himself unable to look up. He did not want to see the flowers again, or hear their tale. He suspected he knew it already, but he did not want their tears to tell him, not now.

Thankfully the chauffeur was at the gate, just walking in.

'So you had to come down to earth finally, huh, *goxai*?' he smirked.

Dino only ground his teeth, not looking at him. And for the whole distance to his house, he kept his eyes directed to the ground, seeing nothing.

❧

As his feet moved mechanically forward, a dark cloud glowered inside Dino's head, clogging his ears, damming his thoughts. He did not even realize when he had crossed the hill and reached the cemetery next to his house. But when he came to, he was seated on a gravestone. It was the same gravestone ('*Name Unknown, Pioneer, Indian Pioneer Corps, Death: 9/8/1945*' it read) he and Tarini had sat upon one evening, about ten days back, reading Nabakanta Barua's poetry. Tarini had brought them there to read the one about the dead moon rising from its grave. He had chosen the spot because it was secluded, situated at the far end of the cemetery where the land started undulating upwards, creating small hillocks that skirted around the Nabagraha Hill.

'*Goxai*,' Tarini had said, 'who needs alcohol when we have poetry to get drunk on?'

'*Hei, hei*,' Dino had chided him then. 'Don't talk about alcohol, Tarini, or we will fall into sin.'

'But you, a *goxai* from the *xattra*, are already deeply in sin, my friend,' Tarini had taunted, 'for you have entered the necropolis of the *boga bongal*, the white man, the foreigner, the *Christian*!'

Dino had walked away in a huff then, and not spoken to Tarini for a couple of days. His friend had wheedled his way back in, though, as he usually did. They were two people alone in a city that was not yet home. They only had each other.

Dino was startled to find himself there again. What was it that had dragged him back there, he wondered. And he felt afraid. He rose to leave but in his haste, he dropped his bag. His stories spilled out. As he was collecting them, his hand brushed against the thorns of the Japanese rose bush that bloomed merrily on the grave of the unknown soldier. He felt his skin smarting. A thin red line appeared on the back of his hand. Droplets of blood.

'Tej,' the word snaked its way into his heart. It was icy cold.

Slinging the bag over his shoulder again, Dino climbed over the broken fence that separated Barua Asthan from the cemetery and hurried back to his room. He closed the door behind him and paced around the room. He sat on his bed, then jumped up. He thought he should empty his bag; check to see he had not lost any of his stories. His hands were shaking slightly when he reached in to retrieve the pages untidily tucked into the bag. A low terrified whimper escaped him when his fingers touched something fleshy inside his bag. He withdrew his hand and emptied the contents onto his bed. He almost laughed out loud when he saw a bunch of pale pink Japanese roses squished between the pages of his stories. And then he cried.

Dino cried and cried and cried. Hugging his knees to his chest, he sat on the floor, rocking back and forth. The tears would not stop.

❧

'*Goxai, oi goxai*!' Tarini's voice woke him up, and the loud thumping on the wall next to his bed. The two of them were 'wall-mates'.

Dino sat up on his bed to see it was almost dark outside. A bright orange sun was sending in the last of its warm rays into his room through the ventilator above the window. He sneezed a couple of times then, for the dust from Tarini's wall thumping was tickling his nose.

'Oh, so you are alive?' Tarini sounded angry. 'I have been trying to wake you up for the past half an hour. I was going to break down the door next.'

'No need. I'm opening it,' Dino called out as he walked towards the door. His whole body was stiff. And he felt hungry. When Tarini appeared in front of his room, he asked, 'Do you have anything to eat?'

'I do. But what happened to you? What happened at the big house? What did the old woman want?'

'I'm hungry. Let's eat and then we can talk.'

If Tarini was put off by Dino's apparent calm, he did not say anything. He went back into his room and returned a little while later with two plates of boiled rice, some fried fish, salt and mustard oil.

'Let's eat in your room,' he suggested.

Dino was leaning against a pillar on the back veranda looking out at the many-hued sky that was slowly being devoured by the darkness of a moonless night. He followed Tarini back to his room.

His friend stopped short, without comment, when he saw the state of Dino's stories, crushed under his weight while he had slept on top of them. Dino watched, motionless, as Tarini placed the food on one corner of the bed, picked up the pages from the bed, and ironing them with his hands, arranged them in a pile on the overcrowded table. Dino's heart beat fast when, suddenly, Tarini noticed the tiny bunch of pink roses on the floor beside the bed and bending down, picked them up and placed them on top of the pile.

When he was done with the pages, Tarini picked up the plates from the bed again. Dino almost snatched his plate from his friend's hand and started stuffing his mouth with large fistfuls of rice.

'What is this, *goxai*? What's happening to you? You must tell me.'

Tarini's voice was shrill with concern.

'I don't know what to tell you,' Dino said, licking his fingers. 'Let's finish our food and then we can talk.'

Dino was stalling and Tarini knew it. But he said nothing.

After they had washed their dishes, they sat down on the bench in the front veranda like they did on most nights. Tarini shifted his weight a little to retrieve from the stained side pockets of his trousers a bunch of tamul-pan wrapped in soggy newspaper.

'I plucked them yesterday,' he said, perhaps hoping to start the conversation.

For a while, the two friends chewed their tamul-pan in silence. Then Tarini stood up to spit out the red juice that oozed out from chewing the mixture of betel nut, betel leaf and white lime. He miscalculated, and instead of falling on the ground below the veranda, most of the red juice was now splattered on the white-washed pillar in front of them. Dino stared at the stain, and kept staring.

'So are you going to say something now?' Tarini tried again.

In some remote corner of his brain, the thought occurred to Dino that his friend's patience with him must have run out.

'She wants me to tutor her son,' he offered.

'*He'll want more*,' said a voice in the same remote corner of his brain.

'And that scares you? Why?'

His friend was not to be fooled.

'*I cannot lie to him. He's my only friend*,' the voice threatened to break free of that precariously controlled zone inside his brain.

Out loud, he said, 'No, but being in that house does.'

'*Why did I say that?*' the voice inside him squealed.

'Why, *goxai*?' Tarini sounded genuinely surprised.

'I don't know,' Dino answered honestly. The voice in his head became quiet.

'Did you hear something? See something out of the ordinary? These big people have bigger secrets than their houses. Did she kill her husband or something, *ha*? She is a strong woman, she could've. Tell me, tell! I always thought it was convenient how he died so soon after the son was born. But then he died here, in this house, you know.'

'How old do you think she is, Tarini?' His friend's feverish outburst awakened something in Dino too and he was suddenly animated.

'Maybe around fifty?' Tarini sounded hopeful. Was this leading somewhere?

'That's not so old in some cultures, no?'

'No, fifty is not old,' said Tarini.

The tone of Dino's voice had suggested he wanted some reassurance.

'But when a woman is married off at fifteen or sixteen, by the time she is forty, she has acquired all the trappings of old age. By fifty, she is ancient, I suppose.'

'Are you thinking about her son? Do you know something I don't? Is he not Xarbessar Barua's son? Whose bastard is he then?' Tarini persisted.

'I don't *know* anything,' Dino said and retreated again.

'*Shhhhhhhhhhh...*'

There was a soft hiss in Dino's head. The picture of a wide-eyed toddler with a finger on his lips peered out at him from the mud wall of somebody's house. Dino was standing in front of a calendar without dates, studying the toddler in the semi-darkness. There was light flickering in from outside. An old woman was seated by the fire outside, telling the gruesome tale of the young girl with a lust for life, her name signifying the life-blood that flowed in her veins. Tej, Tejimola, Tejassini...

Somewhere far away, he heard Tarini sigh. He struggled to come back. He saw deep concern in his friend's eyes.

'Let's go sleep, *goxai.* You don't look so well,' he heard Tarini say. 'Do you want me to sleep in your room? Will you be all right?'

'No, no, Tarini, I'm fine,' Dino assured him.

If his friend caught the feeble note in his voice, he did not react to it. Dino could feel the blood thumping in his veins again, threatening to cut out the air in his lungs.

'Well then, don't latch your door. I'll check in on you if I hear anything to worry me,' Tarini waited for Dino also to rise and let him walk ahead. Dino entered his room and shut the door behind him. Then, he heard his friend's footsteps receding.

When he woke up, nearly a month later, Dino could not at first remember what had happened in the long night that followed. He felt weak and drained. But the memories came trickling back in, slowly.

Kuxumpriya Baruani *baideu*'s chauffeur drove him back to his room a couple of days later, uncharacteristically quiet. Dino was relieved. Ramani *bhakat* had his food ready and was waiting for him in his room. The *bhakat* had looked after him the past few days at the hospital.

'Ramani kaka, when do you leave? Dangor da will need you at the *xattra*,' Dino said between mouthfuls of rice.

'Your Dangor da needs me to be here, so here I am,' the *bhakat* said, simply.

Dino remembered how he had felt at first, seeing the lines of worry on Dangor da's forehead when he had come to visit him at the hospital.

'You are okay?' he had asked authoritatively when Dino had opened his eyes from his drug-induced sleep. One could almost miss the question mark at the end of his sentence.

'Dangor da,' Dino had whimpered, and he had wept again then, like he had wept for the many days and nights past, between his dreams of a young girl, whose mother had stopped loving her because her father would not. He loved her not as a father, but as a man who was not her father.

'Dino, what's happening to you? Stop crying like a girl!' Dangor da's voice was impatient, harsh. It stemmed the tide; he did not want to disappoint his brother.

How then could he tell him, or anybody else for that matter, that he did indeed feel like a girl, *that* girl, whose eyes had haunted him day and night; whose pain had left behind lacerations on his body and soul; whose life-blood had oozed out of *his* being; whose tej, indeed, was his tej.

'What is all this you have been blabbering about to your friend? You have scared him away.'

'Tarini is gone? Where?' Dino asked weakly.

'He got a job last week in Shillong. He left you at the hospital and ran away,' Dangor da said.

'I don't know if you will ever get a job yourself now. Mad people do not get jobs.'

Dangor da's tone hurt Dino. He felt like crying again, but controlled himself. Was he really mad?

'So this is what we are going to do now,' the god among men was taking charge. 'We tell everybody you had fever and delirium. You go prostrate yourself before Kuxumpriya, ask for her forgiveness. Then you pack your bags from her house and shift to Manabendra Goswami's outhouse. You sit for your exams and I will see to it that you get a teaching job at Patkusi. Oh, and stop writing nonsense. I have asked Ramani to burn your stories.'

Dino turned his face to the wall. He pretended to go back to sleep and did not acknowledge Dangor da when he called out to him a few seconds later that he was leaving.

Dino always knew that Dangor da had a huge following among the rich and the famous in Guwahati. Now he realized why. He solved their problems both in the spiritual realm and right here, on this soiled earth. He was a true leader of men, a god on earth. And he, Dino, was nobody, a madman. Society was for normal people. In order to function in society, one would have to act normal, right, even if one was not quite that? Dino determined to follow Dangor da's instructions to the letter.

As he drifted off to sleep again, a little worm started crawling around inside his heart, nibbling its way around. He felt a mild pain and tears stung the inside of his eyelids. He stifled a sob trying to escape his throat. He remembered Puni bai's eyes, those oceans of kindness that had been his refuge throughout his childhood. It had been years now since he had revelled in her love. If only she had not eloped with that good-for-nothing Xarat, she could have come to visit him. Now she was an outcaste in the village. He would be too if he let her so much as touch him. He had wanted his elder brother to touch his hand to his forehead though, and bless him. Maybe if he had not pretended to fall asleep, he would have...

Dino did not want to live in Barua Asthan any longer than was absolutely necessary. He was frightened of the night for he remembered now that during the last few weeks, the nights had brought an endless stream of dreams. He had dreamed of Tejassini, lying on her bed, empty eyes pinned to the ceiling. He had dreamed of the heavy weight she had had thrust upon her, of being her father's daughter. Her father: a good man, who did a lot for the community; everybody loved him. And he loved her, night after night, day after day, until her mother hated her for it. His dreams had led him to wander out of his room to the part of the house where it had all happened, and which had remained locked, forbidding inquiry. Tarini had dragged him back to his room one night after he had woken up to hear his friend trying to break open the lock with a brick.

'*Hei, hei, hei, goxai*, what are you doing?' Tarini had come running down the veranda toward him.

It had taken him an enormous amount of effort to lead Dino back to his room. Dino had resisted, suddenly discovering strange reserves of inhuman strength in himself, but Tarini had always been bigger and stronger than him. For the rest of the night, he had had to be physically restrained. At one point, Tarini had even threatened to tie him to the bed with a rope; only, he could not get himself to do that to his friend. His eyes had shone with sheer horror as he had sat through the night listening to Dino's ramblings.

'He got what he deserved, Tarini, I'm telling you, he got what he deserved...But she should have loved her. Why didn't she love her?'

By the time the sun rose in the morning, Dino had dozed off. He had woken up some time later to find Tarini nodding his head in an uncomfortable sleep, perched on the wooden chair next to his bed. His friend had sat vigil throughout the night.

The mornings had been lucid, Dino remembered. And they had brought with them shame and guilt. He had woken Tarini up then and asked him to go sleep on his own bed. Tarini had refused.

'You will drive me mad too, *goxai*!' he had complained. 'All night I heard your tales of Tejimola dead in childbirth, blossoming back to life, and of purple flowers weeping tears of blood over the gate at the big house. I get what her name means: *kuxum-priya.* What's that got to do with tej, Tejimola, bloody murder?'

Dino had felt shame wash over him in waves as his friend had continued in a petulant voice, 'I blame myself, *goxai.* I should have seen the signs and steered you away. But I was in the throes of my own theatrics about you as this mad genius, this creative genius. You need to give your mind some rest. I will take you to the hospital today. Will you come?'

Dino had gone without protest, and Tarini had never returned. His friend's desertion seemed well deserved to Dino now, but at the hospital, he had had the most gruesome dreams about his fate. Tarini had, after all, promised to be back the next day after he had sent word home through Kuxumpriya Baruani.

'Don't tell her I know,' his parting words to his friend had come out slurred. The drugs were already having their sedative effect...

As he packed his meagre belongings and piled them on to a rickshaw with Ramani *bhakat's* help that evening, he wondered what or how much of his ramblings Tarini had indeed relayed to the matriarch. He guessed from Dangor da's involvement that he must have revealed some of the details, and he dreaded the moment next morning when he would have to come face to face with his former benefactress, taking her leave, asking her forgiveness, as instructed. But he was determined to go through with it, to face his demons, and to emerge victorious.

Dino felt an electric sense of renewal and rejuvenation as he walked down to Kuxumpriya Baruani *baideu*'s house the next morning. He remembered the many cleansing ceremonies he had witnessed at the *xattra* growing up, and realized that, in some ways, he was going through one of them himself. He was, after all, purging his past, and cleansing his soul of the dark and dreadful thoughts that had poisoned him to the point of madness.

He felt ecstatic and he walked briskly.

He was almost at the house now, and he stopped short.

There was new construction underway. The rickety old iron gate was gone. A small muddy path, wide enough for one person to pass by at a time, had been left in the center of what used to be the gate earlier. And on either side of this path, were two deep gaping holes. Sturdy iron rods embedded in a cement base were sticking out of the holes.

The creeper was gone. The flowers were gone. Tejassini-Tejimola was gone.

She must be floating in the river.

Dino turned around hastily and started walking back.

He had to reach the river.

Never Got Written

This would have been an extraordinary story. A kickass, heart-wrenching, tear-jerking, life-altering, award-winning story.

But it never got written.

❧

One day. 4.45 a.m.

It came to the writer in the morning one day as she sat at her trash-picked writing desk staring at the blinking cursor on the blank screen of her laptop. Of late, she had been doing this a lot. She had come to America to complete her short fiction manuscript. She only had a year left on her fellowship, and here she was, struggling to complete the last story.

She had written five of the stories before she left India: that was how she got the fellowship. But since coming to America, she had written only three more that she thought were good enough.

'*Just one more, and I'll wrap it up,*' she had decided finally. But that one final story remained elusive.

'*Come to me, please, come to me!*' she pleaded now, again.

The concluding story had to be different but telling, connected to and connecting the ones that had come before.

She had tried out a few that came to her, but abandoned them halfway through, or one-third of the way through, or even after just a sentence or a paragraph. None of them felt quite like the one to leave her reader with.

All through teaching her fiction writing class at the university and attending workshops and readings at the department, or dropping her eight-year-old at the bus stop and picking him up, taking him for his after-school soccer lessons and coding classes, or cooking for the two of them and cleaning the apartment, she waited for *the* story to come. It never did.

This summer, she was determined to finish writing her manuscript. Workshopping, revising, and pitching publishers would take long enough, but if she did not have the draft manuscript ready, the book would take even longer to see the light of day. The terms of the fellowship required her to submit only the final draft; getting it published while still in the US was her dream. She felt that if she could not build the required networks in the publishing industry while being at one of the most prestigious—and resource-rich—university writing programs in the country, she might as well give up being a writer.

'*I have to get a desk*,' she had decided, as a first step.

The university did not provide office space to visiting fellows. Three days a week, when she was not teaching and meeting students at the Starbucks across from the picturesque Victorian townhouse that was the Writing Department, she would write at home sitting on a bar stool on the kitchen island. Her neck muscles would start straining after a few minutes, and the pain shooting through her spine would trigger in her brain the image of a pair of frenzied eyes that she locked on to just before she hurtled against the Moroccan Blue wall of her bedroom with a force that left her bedridden for three months nearly seven years ago. She would have to abandon her writing then, stretch her muscles like her physiotherapist back home in Guwahati had taught her, and if that did not help, go get the painkillers.

'*I don't want drug dependency added to the list of allegations he's made against me in court*,' she determined.

And so, last week, she picked a desk from the dumpster behind the building. And an office chair and another comfy chair for her living room.

'*Who throws away such good furniture?*' she mumbled, running her hand over the desk's rugged walnut surface and feeling its uneven texture grazing her palm.

Last year, when she first arrived, she had seen people from the neighbouring apartments in the bi-college area picking up pieces of furniture from the garbage dump after the international students dropped them there at the end of the school year. Her neighbour, Jennifer, told her later that rather than pay the city to pick them up or hazard being duped (or worse) by weirdos on Craigslist, the online store, the students dumped these lightly used pieces; anybody could pick them up if they needed.

'Just don't pick up beds and mattresses. They might have bed bugs,' she warned.

Back in India, she could never have imagined using furniture discarded by anyone else. Or picking anything from a dumpster. Scavenging was for poor people in a country where the not-poor reused branded plastic shopping bags till the logos on them faded but felt offended when offered a pair of Levi's jeans their cousin had outgrown. 'We can buy our own, we're not poor,' they would say.

'*Well, I am poor here*,' she had said to herself as she dragged the furniture pieces one by one to the elevator.

Once, she had carefully curated the furniture that would not clash with the Moroccan Blue living room wall and would complement the colours that she picked for the rest of the walls of the house she had purchased with her husband in Delhi. She had paid for it to be delivered and assembled at home. Then six years ago one day, she left it all behind, moved a thousand miles away from her husband—from the city she'd made her home in after marriage to the one she'd spent her childhood in—choosing her life, and her son's, over her possessions. In the next few years, she had built a new life for herself and her son, from scratch. New job, new responsibilities, new home. It helped that her parents were close by to support her when she needed them. And now, she was building up again, but alone in a new country. She had had to leave again because the distance of a thousand miles had not been enough to shield her from her husband's hurt ego. How dare she continue to survive without him controlling every aspect of her life?

Well, in this country, she was barely managing. Her meagre stipend barely covered her rent and groceries. She had had to dip in to her savings several times, and they were fast disappearing, what with a child to raise on wages that were meant for a single adult willing to rough it out for the prestige of being associated with an Ivy Plus. Additionally, her legal expenses back home were piling up. Being away from the country while still fighting a legal battle with her husband over divorce and custody six years after she left him meant paying her lawyers to represent her and file several legal petitions on her behalf, just to reassure the courts that she had not run away, but was only trying to advance her career for the sake of a better life for her child who she was raising singlehandedly, without any financial support from her husband.

'*But on the other hand, we are safe here, physically,*' she rationalized as she rode the elevator up to the fourth floor. '*That's at least $100 saved,*' she smiled even as she panted and puffed, arranging the desk and office chair in one corner of the living room and the comfy chair in another, by the floor lamp.

'*I have a reading nook* and *a writing station!*'

As she surveyed the room from her kitchenette, she felt incredibly hopeful.

But neither curling up on her comfy chair nor sitting upright, alert and expectant, at her writing desk had helped her move that blinking cursor forward to fill the blank page on the screen with words from her story.

This had happened every day for the past five days.

On a school day, she would wake up at 4.30 a.m., make herself a cup of green tea, and start up her laptop. This way, she could put in at least two hours of work before she had to make breakfast and lunch for Tej, wake him up, get him ready for school, and finally take him to the bus stop, after which she herself would either rush to catch the 8.20 to University City, or settle down at the kitchen counter to get enough writing done to justify her residence in the country. If she was home, she saved the hour she otherwise spent on commute. And despite having to jump off the bar stool every fifteen minutes or so to do some calisthenics or pop a pill before climbing up again, she would squeeze in some writing between prepping for her class, grading her students, and replying to the 101 emails in her inbox from people at the university, ninety-nine of which could probably have been quick conversations in the hallway when they had passed each other the day before.

Today, she was home. She had her desk and office chair, her grading was done, the semester over, and Tej's school would not break for the summer until next week. While he was at school, she would have all day to do the rest of the less soul-wrenching work, like editing. But the early hours had always been her time apart from time. While the rest of the world clung on to the last morsels of sleep and forgetting, her characters would emerge from that liminal space between memory and invention, truth and telling, to interact with her most animatedly. Her first drafts usually came to her during these hours of the dawn and early morning. Later in the day, when the world went busily about its business, it was easy to revisit her work with a critical eye to edit it, polish it, and present it to the world in a way that would make it laugh or cry, and love or hate, her characters.

But she had been sitting at her desk every day for the past five days with no success, making false starts, deleting, digressing, disintegrating.

Her cup of tea sat steaming beside her laptop. Ignoring it, she turned back to her blank screen and blinking cursor.

But the cup would not be ignored. She could smell the faint smell of the jasmine tea that she had settled on this morning because she had run out of 'real' tea. A grocery store run was long overdue. She made a mental note to go to the Indian store later today, crushing the urge to walk up to the fridge and add 'Assam tea' to the grocery list stuck to its side.

'*I'll add it later. Or I'll be writing the grocery list for the rest of the morning. Can't drink this artificial tea another day, so I won't forget*,' she assured herself.

Again, that tantalizing, sweet, sickening smell of jasmine. If the online grocery store had not delivered the jasmine tea in error, she would never have bought it. Now she had to drink it. She scowled at it.

'*You do realize I haven't written a single word yet, don't you? What's the point of waking up at 4 a.m. to write if all I do is make tea that is not tea, drink it, and stare at the screen? And now I need biscuits*!'

Two years in America and she still called them biscuits, not cookies. She blamed it on her neighbour who had lived in apartment 5B across the hall. She was British, Bangladeshi but British. She had been her only friend in the building till she moved out four months ago. Now the writer only talked to inanimate things, like her cup of tea. She needed real people to talk to, like Seher, who would tell her she should get on with her writing or get a swift kick in the ass.

She had half lifted that ass from her chair to go get her biscuits when she felt herself being firmly, and with a force that was almost physical, pushed back down into the chair.

'*Write me*,' said a voice in her ear.

The tea and biscuits dissipated from their lived and longed for existences respectively. Her hands moved instinctively to her keyboard. But her fingers did not know where to go or how to move over its surface.

'*Tell me how I should write you.*' Her ears burned, her heart thrummed.

'*I'm just the story.* You *are my writer. I'm here. Make me outstanding,*' commanded the voice from behind her.

She felt it breathing against her ear. She shivered. Abruptly, the memory of a pair of pink-brown lips brushing against her lobe drenched her. Those lips had been at the nape of her neck. Soon they would be on her lips: her first kiss. She vaguely remembered that a pair of hands were also involved—not hers—that rested either on her shoulders or over her breasts, or under. Her muscles had clenched in deep, dark places, just as they were clenching now. But there were no hands now, just the breath. And a voice that fell into place the moment it spoke.

'*You're here.*'

'*You're flushed,*' said the voice from behind her.

'I have to go to the bathroom, Ma!'

The warmth drained from the writer's body as she instinctively turned to the voice from the doorway.

'Good morning, *deha*! It's almost time to get up and get ready for school anyway. Let's get you to the bathroom first!'

She shut the laptop screen and pushed back her chair. No voice pulled her back this time, no breath followed her.

Another day. 3.47 p.m.

'I'm watching you from over there, okay?'

The writer refused to let the judgemental gaze of all the other parents on the playground pull her back as she left Tej on the slide and made her way toward the blanket she had spread out earlier on the soft grass under the most beautiful copper beech in the sprawling park. She lay down on it now and covered her face with her scarf to keep the sun from hurting her eyes, but through the thin muslin, she could still see the purple leaves above her squinting at the sunlight.

'*At his age I was walking to school alone, keeping my eyes on the ground as Ma said to, so I didn't get raped by some soldier from the Indian Army. Tej will be fine being on his own a few feet away from me. This is not a conflict zone. I haven't abandoned him. I even got us a picnic dinner. I haven't slept in three nights, I'm exhausted, and I deserve some rest!*'

'*You're probably doing your best,*' her story said unconvincingly. It was clearly disappointed at not being written yet, and lay listlessly beside her.

A teardrop stood poised at the corner of her right eye, ready to roll down the moment she blinked.

'*Probably? No, probably not. Everyone else I know is publishing in prestigious journals and landing literary agents and winning awards. Last week, I couldn't even make it to the panel discussion at the writing center; Judy wanted me there to meet with the agents and editors she invited. But I would not have reached home in time to meet Tej's school bus. So I didn't go. Then I missed the deadline for that award she wanted to nominate me for, if only I could put together all the documents they'd asked for. I was busy looking after a sick child. Judy's been an amazing faculty associate, but I've not been a good mentee. There are other mothers out there, writing and publishing, living a life. Why can't I?*'

On Monday, Tej had come home with a fever. The school year had only just started and the petri dish of diseases that it was, it had already succumbed to the changing season to send fever and flu home with the kids. Before him, it was Alexander from the bus: for almost a week, the writer had missed her two-minute morning catch-ups with his mom at the stop.

'Jennifer will have lots to say about this week's Tinder dates when we meet next,' she had sighed as she stood at the window and watched the bus pull away from their stop the next day. Two years after her husband had died in a freak accident involving an icy road and a woman who was not her, Jennifer was exploring her options in the world of men again.

'I get lonely and they're not all bad,' she had sounded apologetic.

The writer had hugged her then, 'Do what makes you feel good about yourself again.'

'*I'm lonely too*,' she admitted to herself now as she made pancakes for Tej: it was almost morning when the poor child had fallen asleep after being up all night with a clogged nose, gasping for breath. She lay beside him for an hour trying to catch a nap so she could function during the day, but sleep would not come. She had woken up her laptop then to email Judy about finding someone to sub for her class. And then remained glued to the laptop for the next hour or two, responding to student emails, paying her internet and electricity bills, and signing Tej up for winter classes to keep him busy while school was out. If she signed him up now, she would get an early bird price. She could use the money this saved to pay a babysitter if she finally managed to go to one of the writing/publishing events coming up at the university.

'*All that's left now is to schedule our flu shots and find out when I have to take Tej for his annual pediatrician's visit,*' she reminded herself.

'*Why don't you write me now?*' The story was persistent.

'*I'm tired, and I want to sleep for the next ten days. But all I'm doing is mending one hole in my boat while it springs another hole on the other side of it which I'd thought I'd already mended. You being in my head all the time is not helping. And not just my head, but in the space around me. Enveloping me, embracing me, squeezing the breath out of me. You also are exhausting me!*'

'*Hey, it's okay, I won't abandon you!*'

She wished she could cry then, but there had been no time for tears in the past six years, and sometimes, she could not remember how she used to cry at all.

'*If—when—I cry, I will cry gracefully, with tears flowing down my cheeks in a straight line, like in the movies. I won't cry messily, rubbing snot and tears all over my face. And you can't make me cry now: I'm hungry. Soon Tej will wake up hungry. But here I am, once again, talking to a story!*'

She knew these were silly, cringe-worthy thoughts. Maybe not talking to real people did that to you. These days, on the rare occasion that she did have a conversation with another adult, she mostly listened. She realized she had been doing this for a while now.

When Seher was living across the hallway from her in their moldy suburban apartment building, they had spent a lot of time together, drinking cup after cup of tea. Her friend talked endlessly as they dunked biscuits in their cups and picked up the soggy bits at the bottom with a teaspoon at the end. She talked about her girls, how it was great that they now had Tej as a little brother to play with, about her parents and friends spread out on different continents across the globe, and how they all kept asking her to come live with them and how that would stifle her, but most of all, she talked about her husband.

'Wankers these men are!' Seher would say, and narrate another story of how her 'baldy' made her feel like shit throughout their marriage. The writer would listen, and remember how her husband would also make her feel like shit and then, beat the shit out of her, leaving her feeling nothing. But she would not say any of this to her friend. Right now, her friend needed her to listen, and she would.

In any case, she did not talk much about her marriage to people anymore. She stopped after she realized it only elicited well-meaning advice on what she should have done to prevent the abuse and how she should deal with the trauma now that she had left it behind. Instead, she just wrote about it, like she wrote about how she would stiffen at the sight of any man in uniform and dream at night of walking to school, eyes closed, stumbling over what could be rocks or body parts of people mixed with bits of the fish and meat and vegetables that blew up with the bomb in the marketplace. They all heard the bomb go off and the living room window had a small crack that was not big enough to require replacement, and anyway, it made for good conversation for years after.

'See this crack here? That's how powerful the bomb was. My fishmonger died. I could have been buying my mid-week fish from him. But I stayed home to grade exam papers,' her father would say as he led all guests to the window.

'That's the highlight of your father's pathetic, unexciting life?' Rajesh had scoffed when first introduced to the window story. He had definitely made her life so much more exciting, only the cracks in her could not be seen on the outside.

She had gone against her parents' wishes to get married to a mainlander; he was never going to understand what it was like growing up in a militarized hinterland, made peripheral and expendable. Well, at least he gave her continuity: with him, she had traded the everyday violence of racial slurs and bomb blasts and extra-judicial killings and rape and molestation that she experienced and/or witnessed growing up for more racial slurs and forced sex and beatings inside the bedroom and, on that day that she finally walked out, strangulation.

The day her father died, she had tried to dig her nails into the pane where the crack was, but the surface was smooth.

'*Maybe if we both just shattered, we could be fixed and made whole again*,' she said to the window. But the window held itself together so that her mother could now take over the storytelling.

Stories keep people from disintegrating, by holding the pieces together.

'That is why I write,' she had said in her fellowship application. A writer from a conflict zone who wrote about intersecting personal and political violences. She had made a compelling case and they had paid her to come here and write.

'*But not enough to afford therapy here, and if I see a shrink in India, Rajesh will tell the court I'm mad and take Tej away.*'

The three days that Tej was home with the flu had been filled with heartbreaking hugs and dire threats of '*swallow your medicine and inhale that steam*', and very little sleep and a lot of regret at time slipping by unproductively, some red-hot anger at the person she held responsible for her current situation, and a lot of bitterness at a life that would not relent. But then, she would take a sideways glance at the little person sleeping in his corner of the bedroom, wheezing, and her insides would unclench a little, the blackness would let in some ashen, pale light, and she would breathe easier, just a little.

She had sent him to school today and as she watched him run home from the bus, she knew he was back to being the bundle of energy that exhausted her with its limitless exuberance and kept her hyperactive up until the time she lay down on her bed and blacked out while it prattled on in the other bed.

'Let's get us some Vitamin D,' she had said to him and they had walked down to the park.

Most days she enjoyed the twenty-minute walk to the park. Tej loved pushing the call buttons on all the traffic lights after every block on the way and she enjoyed the walk-stop, walk-stop rhythm. Living in this sleepy suburban town sometimes made her nostalgic for a Guwahati that might have been when her parents first made their home there: a city where people were not squeezed in tight and the houses could breathe in the scent of the flowers growing in the grounds outside, where you took the time to greet strangers you walked past with a smile (even if it did not always reach your eyes), and there was a quiet that you could retrieve when you needed despite the chaos of everyday city life. Hiking in the surrounding hills or crossing the river into the city by train now, she would be reminded of the

Guwahati she lived in in her mind during her years growing up there: a green city lazing by a mighty big river, carrying the reassuring weight of a broken string of small hills on its bosom.

She knew these hills were where poor people like her parents built their first bamboo houses till they could establish themselves enough to afford a concrete house in the plains. Meanwhile, the rich people lived in their big concrete houses at the foot of these hills till they could amend the environmental laws enough to build their gaudy mansions on the hilltops or the riverfront. She had watched the people moving up and down, down and up, as the bombs started going off, and the anti-insurgency money started flowing in, and people got distracted from community building and political activism by big buildings and blinding lights, while their protest chants and slogans drowned in the noise of cars honking angrily and loud religious music blaring out on every street.

When she remembered her city that was several continents away, though, she only remembered the good things, because this place where she found herself in now was good at ignoring the bad stuff. Like why two cops walked into the Indian store on the other side of Main Street and picked up a Black teenager who had stopped to buy a pack of cigarettes after putting his brother on the school bus. The brother, Jeremiah, was in Tej's homeroom, and the boys' mom recounted the next day when the writer met her at the school play how he had been dropped back home in a couple of hours, with much apologizing.

'You have a strapping young lad here: it's easy to mistake him for a grown man,' they had laughed.

'And don't go owing money to mean shop owners no more,' they cautioned Jeremiah's brother good-naturedly and left a keychain with a LED torchlight and a plastic hat with the PD logo on it for Jeremiah.

When the writer told Jennifer all about it the next morning, she bristled.

'This is why we need to defund the police. They picked him up simply based on a complaint, without verifying the facts, because he is Black and lives on the other side of the tracks!'

She wanted to say there was that—and more—to think about when addressing racism in America, or anywhere really, but then she remembered how on their last playdate, Alexander had asked Tej to come to his house because, 'I don't like the way the food smells at your place.' Jennifer had laughed at how kids would say the darndest thing, even to their best mates, and asked the writer to join them for dinner when she came to pick Tej up after the playdate. She had agreed readily because not only would she save the two hours when the boys played together but also the hour and a half that she would otherwise spend cooking and feeding the child and cleaning and washing up after. She had planned on watching an A-rated war movie for a change, with a glass of wine in hand, when she got home, but was snoring on the couch before the gory battles started.

'*I can't doze off now, here in the park*,' she scolded herself. She had had maybe ten hours of sleep over the last five days, and what was usually a pleasant walk to the park, especially at this time of the year, had been particularly challenging today with a picnic meal and blanket to carry while also shepherding a little human.

'*How am I going to do this? For how long?*'

She felt the teardrop hanging from the corner of her eye grow saltier.

'*Let's brainstorm on how I'll begin writing you,*' she tried to involve the story, hoping for distraction.

'*You can't write me when you're like this. Just breathe!*'

She did, and a green smell rushed inside her lungs.

Once she had run away from home after a fight with her mother and hidden herself in a small clearing among some thick bushes on a clifftop behind the house. She did not feel it would be prudent to venture too far away; the army or the insurgents could be hiding in the thicker foliage further out. But this place was perfect because she could see the house from here without herself being seen, and she had hidden herself here before, reading books that she was not meant to be reading. But she had never been here in the dusk, when the light was fading, leaving the river below looking like a neon grey ribbon. Somewhere, not very far away, a fox howled and she inhaled deeply. The smell of the grass on which she lay now made her aware once again that every smell comes with its own colour and fresh green has its own smell.

No one had come to fetch her home that day, and the fox had forced her to abandon her rebellion before anyone could miss her. She had made her own way home.

'*Like I have to now. I wish there were no colours and no smells in this world. If I cannot write about any of it, why give it to me? Just turn everything monochromatic! But then I'd be compelled to write about that too, huh? Compelled, but in no condition to.*'

She sat up to go fetch Tej from the playground, and as

she removed the scarf from her face, it soaked up that lone tear drop hovering at the corner of her eye.

Yet another day. 7.29 p.m.

She wanted to be alone when she cried. She did not want Tej to see her cry. But when you are one of the two people in a small one-bedroom apartment, despite your best efforts, your meltdowns are sometimes likely to happen during the other person's waking hours, when they were home from school.

After all, bad news did not always look for a time convenient to you to reach you, and even if you tried to work around the inconvenience and shelved it for now so that you could deal with it later, it would gestate quietly inside of you and feed your trauma, and noiselessly—like on the sands of a Zen garden—rake up the memories you thought had flattened with the mud of your life, and wake you up and shake you out of the sense of well-being that you had precariously started building around your existence and your kid's.

That moment of awakening came without notice, and sometimes, the writer could successfully lock herself away in the bathroom which was, ironically, the place she was frantic to escape from the day her husband had locked her up and tried to strangle her. These days, when she felt herself breaking down, she often retreated to the bathroom, to sit on the cold floor and catch her breath as life whooshed around outside the door, calling her name, knocking on the door, and asking 'How much longer?' Today, it came in the middle of attending to a heated pan on the stove which could not be turned off or there would be no dinner tonight.

She was not even aware that the tears were rolling down her cheeks, because she had not really cried in years. Her meltdowns usually brought asthmatic wheezing, sharp words, and loud wails which she had learned to tame by inhaling salbutamol, shrieking into a bath towel, and/or lying down on the white bathroom floor that she cleaned obsessively every day: the cold tiles helped freeze the outbursts, so that by the time she was ready to open the door and step back out into the world of kid talk and parental responsibilities, she would have less guilt weighing her down. And although she never felt the universe listening to her, today, her tears came just the way she had wanted them to: rolling down in straight lines over both cheeks without making a mess.

She realized she was crying when she felt a tear drop on her wrist as she leaned in to taste the salt in the vegetables she was stirring in the pan.

'*I'm crying*,' was her first reaction.

'*I can't cry now*,' was the next.

'Ma, I'm hungry,' came the loud voice of the little person from the living room.

'We'll eat in ten, okay? Finish your drawing.'

The panic in her voice was probably only apparent to her, but she frantically wiped the tears with her sleeve and furiously stirred the vegetables, as though the cooking was the cause and the food to blame.

'*I. Hate. Cooking*!' she deflected, but the words from the email that had reached her last night started suddenly, mechanically, playing in a loop in her head, heavy against her ears. It had arrived last night, just as she was falling asleep.

'*Why did I have to check my email on the phone*?'

She had cursed herself for deviating from her self-imposed

rule of not using her phone as a laptop. But the exhaustion of the day had put her to sleep anyway. She had woken up late in the morning, having uncharacteristically turned off the first alarm of the day. She remembered telling herself groggily that she would not be able to write today anyway, though she had not remembered why she had slept fitfully throughout the night. When she woke up with the second alarm to get Tej ready for school, her day had picked up its usual pace and occupied the conscious, working space in her brain that kept her running from bus stop to train station (with a quick chat about Jennifer's new boyfriend thrown in for relief); riding the thirty minutes to work in the city, sandwiched between commuters who had piled on to her usual Quiet Ride because the earlier train had been cancelled; taking the bus instead of her refreshing twenty-minute walk to the department because her feet refused to carry her; spending the rest of the day in a blur teaching, meeting with students, attending a departmental meeting, checking out books from the library, figuring out which building in the sprawling campus housed the administrative department that could tell her when her next fellowship installment was coming in, and bumping into a Conflict Studies professor who had been telling her they needed to meet over coffee one day to discuss possible dates for her to read her work at the center he headed.

She had been putting him off because their events were on Mondays and Thursdays, in the evenings, and on a school night, she could not afford to bring Tej with her, attend the entire event, and train it back home before his bedtime. When he missed his bedtime, Tej would not fall asleep till very late and it was always a struggle to get him ready for school the next day. The tiredness she felt on those days was less physical, more soul-crushing: putting up with the early morning tantrum and calming him down in time to meet the bus would drain her to the point that she would need to sit and stare into space for a long, long time before her mind or her body would stir again. By this time, she would have missed her train, if she was going to the university that day and that in turn would upend her entire day; or if she was to sit at home and write, she would probably only be able to write emails.

Today, she did not have a ready excuse when their paths crossed on campus and he was done for the day, and she had an hour before her next class. So, they walked together to the Starbucks to discuss the proposed reading.

'This is the first time I'm doing an impromptu meeting with anyone here. Usually, I have to email for an appointment weeks ahead, even if we work across the hallway from each other.'

He had laughed then, the corners of his amber eyes crinkling. A part of her brain registered the fact, another swept it away.

'I've seen too much of the chaos in the world to want to fit into prescribed patterns of behaviour. People like you and me, who have seen conflict and violence from up close, we are the blue-collar academics. We can adjust to the demands of the situation. Those in their intellectual ivory towers can never improvise.'

'And yet, you are here.'

'And yet, I am here. And I conform too. With them. Not with you. I read what you write.'

She had felt a dull pain in her chest then, a pain that

came with a familiar darkness. If she let it, the darkness would grow, she knew. So she crumpled it and stowed it away in that undefined space where she also sent images of crinkled amber eyes, sensations of soft feather touches during casual conversations, and the fleeting smell of mild aftershave to die. Only sometimes they did not die. Like the email from last night, they sometimes came back to invade her soul, her space, and the semblance of sanity she had built for herself outside of the graveyard of her mind.

In the end, they had decided she would do the reading at the Conflict Studies Center on the Thursday before Fall Break and Tej would miss school on Friday.

'We'll call it a snow day,' she smiled at him.

'Keeping the child out of school for one day does not make you a bad mother. Let him sleep in for a day—in any case, our schools start too early for little kids.'

On the way back from the city and later, in the playground with Tej, she had only thought about what she would read that day, and how she could engage the audience with her work. The email had lain in the graveyard, gathering strength, waiting to assault her when she least expected.

'*Please, please, give me just an hour more. I'll deal with you after Tej is in bed,*' she pleaded, still wiping away those tears. Strangely there were only the tears, no feelings of pain or hurt twisted her insides out of shape as they usually did.

'*Maybe I'm healing, getting over that wanker, not being affected by him anymore,*' she thought hopefully, but not convincingly, as she watched Tej eat in front of the television. The tears had eventually stopped, but she was not ready for Tej yet. Letting him watch television was the only way to keep him disengaged from her.

'*Or maybe the hurt will come later, in oceans rather than rivers,*' she shuddered.

And as it often happened in her head these days, there also appeared a parallel and overlapping thought: '*Seher would be so proud I said/thought/used the word 'wanker'.*'

And another: '*Wow! I don't even have to smoke weed to have these layers upon layers of thought smothering me.*'

Then another: '*You're deflecting. Stop!*'

The feeling of apprehension that was at the center of this maelstrom in her mind pulled her back, and stayed with her as she led Tej to his bed earlier than usual. The boy understandably put up a fight, screaming and protesting. But she was only thinking of herself and how she needed him asleep before she allowed the waves to engulf her.

'*Let me not lose it now,*' she prayed.

'GO. TO. SLEEP!' she yelled out loud, 'Or no playground for you tomorrow.'

Tej was still whimpering when she left the room to lie down on the living room couch to wait for those waves. They did not come.

She waited, holding her breath.

'*I was mean to the boy. Oh, but what will we do now?*'

The email had come from her lawyer in Guwahati, informing her that her husband had filed another civil suit against her, this time to have her passport impounded because she had 'kidnapped' the child and taken him to another country.

'I can hold him off and petition to have your appearance exempted for a few months till you finish your fellowship. But once you return, be prepared to fight him again. Meanwhile, you will need to sign the attached affidavits and other documents and get them notarized…' her lawyer's email read.

'He calculated his timing to coincide with the last stage of my fellowship, knowing it will shake me up and affect my final performance,' she told her lawyer on the phone a couple of hours later, when it was a decent enough time in the morning in India.

'Of course!' her lawyer agreed. 'Why else would he have waited over a year to do this? He also knows that none of this will hold up in court; we had all the legal permissions and court orders in place before you left. It's just the inconvenience of it.'

'It's not just the inconvenience, Ritika. It is also the emotional toll, and the financial cost, and the psychological disruption. And my kid! What happens if he manages to take him away from me?'

'Let's not start panicking! When you start thinking rationally again, you will remember that the law is on our side, even though the legal system in our country has a thousand and one loopholes that people like Rajesh have been exploiting. And as your friend, I have always been honest with you: I told you these litigations can drag on for years, especially when someone as vindictive and petty as your husband is involved. You will have to find your own closure here: the day you start looking at your legal problems as minor inconveniences and background noises—and not as defining, traumatic events of your life—you will find peace.'

'As always, I'm not convinced by your prescription for finding peace, but thank you for being my friend,' the writer half-smiled as she disconnected.

Ritika had said nothing new, and if the same old

approach she had used over the last seven years to deal with Rajesh's continued legal and extra-legal harassment would still hold, she told herself that she did not have to worry about it till she returned to India, or till he sent another threat, legal or otherwise, her way.

'*So then, tomorrow morning, you write me?*' the story asked expectantly as she lay down on her bed finally.

'*I stayed up late to talk to Ritika. I had such a turbulent day today. How do you expect me to write you tomorrow?*'

'*I will never get written,*' said the story and it turned its back to her.

'*You will! I just need a good cry first.*'

'*Cry then. I'm here. I'll hold you,*' said her story, as it rolled back toward her and pulled her closer.

Today. Now.

'*If only you were real!*' she said wistfully.

'*I'm not real because you can't touch me? Don't you feel me with you, in you, every minute, every day?*'

Once, when things had gotten really heated with Rajesh and he had hit her and she lay balled up on the bed whimpering, she had suddenly, very forcefully, and quite incompatibly with the mood of the moment, remembered that wild onrush of feelings one feels when one falls inevitably in love with another: the awareness of them constantly against your skin, on your tongue, in your guts, even when they were miles away, being flooded by their warmth, sensing their breath against your cheek making your eyelids droop, your thighs clench, and your legs curl up to your chest.

She had cried torrential tears then.

'I'll never feel that again!'

And yet, here she was feeling it again, and again, every day, despite her best efforts at ignoring the discomfort it caused as she waved goodbye to Jennifer at the bus stop in the morning, or sprinted across campus between classes, or stepped out of the train on the way back from work, or dusted the living room or went grocery shopping or watched Tej on the playground. It was most debilitating on the days when she was home and supposed to be writing, having missed her self-imposed summer deadline anyway. She would curl up on the comfy chair and scroll through her social media feed without any of it really registering with her, but because it stopped her thinking and feeling for the while. Then she would once again check the messages on her phone, and not finding the one she waited for, put her phone down exasperatedly. She would pick it up again though and scroll through the older messages and feel her face relax and eyes stretch in a smile and her breath stop. And there would be that same feeling overwhelming her again, only more strongly than before.

'*But that's not you, that's an actual human person who's out there,*' she corrected the story.

'Are you sure he is not in your imagination, just as I am?'

'Could he have texted me if he was?'

'So you fell in love with a bunch of words? And that's more real than a story? How do you imagine a story without words?'

'But he is a different story, not you.'

'Then tell me this story that's not me.'

The first text had come about four months back from a reader who said he loved reading her story about the women who would not die, that had just been published in an online journal.

'You blended together the folktales I grew up hearing my father read to me.'

She was not much in the public eye as a writer, and very infrequently on social media. So when someone reached out to her about her work, she knew they had genuinely connected with her words and not her image (what image?).

Writer and reader had texted back and forth, with the reader opening up a new way for her to look at her own writing: through the perspective of someone who was familiar with the context of the stories through intergenerational cultural transmission but who had never been physically immersed in the context as she had been. He was a second generation American; his father was from Assam. They had discussed the idea of home and the nostalgia they felt for a homeland they carried within them but interpreted in different ways.

Then one day, he texted: 'I'm gonna say it: I love you.'

She had frozen and did not reply for a few hours. In the end, because it was rude to ghost people, she sent several smiley emojis and a few 'ha ha ha's'.

'Why do you laugh?' he texted back.

'Because you are confusing me with my writing. You won't even like me when you meet me.'

'Let me decide. Come on a date.'

'I don't do dates. My life is too messed up to meet people. Let's just talk on text.' Another smiley.

And they had continued texting every day. They talked books, music, movies, books, and more books. Till one day, about two months ago, she had woken up in the morning and been unable to leap to her feet like she did every morning when the alarm sounded. She just lay on her bed, weightless, thoughtless, watching beams of bright light filtering in through the blinds letting her know it must have snowed heavily last night.

'Why do I feel good?' she was suspicious.

Suddenly, her insides clenched, and she waited for the usual sense of dread and foreboding to envelop her. Instead, she felt a warmth oozing out of her body. Her breath stopped, her chest heaved, and she picked up her phone to message the reader.

'Are you awake?' she texted and waited.

'The day I decided to let him in and give myself a chance at loving again, he disappeared. He's been ghosting me ever since. I even tried calling a couple of times.'

'What changed?'

'I guess he became a real boy.'

'And the real boy doesn't love you?'

'I guess not.'

'Can you love a real boy?'

'But I do! I'm filled with love, and longing. I feel lighter, like I've shed the darkness I've been carrying around with me for so long. I keep checking my phone, wanting him to be real, imagining I can tell him I love him.'

'Even though he ghosted you?'

'Even though he ghosted me. It only matters that I can love again.'

'Would you consider loving him, or letting him love you if he wasn't just his words but an actual human sitting across the table from you, over a cup of coffee?'

'...'

'So, he is in your imagination. He is real like your

imagination. Like me. I am him; we are both words, the same words.'

'What about the desire? The longing? The wanting? The physical ache?' She had to protest. He could not have not existed.

'Desire is imagination, imagination desire.'

'You've been with me longer than he has.'

'I've been in you so long, maybe I manifested.'

The story was being cheeky. The writer persisted.

'But a story must have an ending. He did not end our story.'

'You are the writer, write your own.'

'What if I left it open, though? Who knows where it might lead?'

'It might lead to fresh new surprises every day, like with Rajesh,' the story was impatient again. *'At some point, you start controlling how your trauma affects you. You leave a wound open, it festers.'*

'And if you close it, that's that,' the writer was desperate now.

'No, if you close it, you move on, you heal.'

There was no winning.

'You sound like Ritika. What if the pain helps me write?'

'What if the healing helps you understand your pain better, write a more layered story?'

'Are you the better story?'

'You will never know until you write me. And you will definitely not get over all the ghosts in your life unless you commit them to words on a page.'

'Then maybe you'll remain a ghost. Maybe you'll never get written.'

'Or maybe I will, because maybe someday, soon, you will heal.'

Acknowledgements

People showed up in my life with flashes of light and moments of love and kindness at the times when everything about life seemed dark and overwhelming. Some stayed awhile, some left immediately; some I did not even recognize while they were there, helping me cope, survive, thrive. I thank them all, for without them, this book would never get written.

The characters in the book are real people: only fiction can tell us the truth about real, everyday people. I thank them for populating my pages.

And mostly, I thank my editor, Renuka Chatterjee, for not giving up on working with me. Her faith in my writing inspires me. I took a long time putting this book together, and I'm glad I'm doing it with her.